EAT THE PUDDING FIRST

A MODERN-DAY RECIPE FOR BUSINESS SUCCESS

GARY ASHWORTH

K
N
O
W
N

www.get-known.co.uk

"

THERE'S SELDOM SUCH A THING

AS AN UNACHIEVABLE GOAL;

JUST AN OVER-AMBITIOUS

TIMETABLE.

"

THIS BOOK IS FOR...

This book has been written for two distinct groups of people:

1. People already running their own businesses, who want to grow earnings and profits at a much more dramatic rate. Perhaps you are wondering how to gear up without risking all you have achieved so far, or have found a successful model you want to replicate again and again. Either way, you may need to work out a new plan and find a different team of helpers for this next part of the journey.

2. People who would like to start their own business but aren't quite sure where or how they should start. Perhaps you haven't decided which type of business you should focus on yet, or haven't been courageous enough to make the first leap? However, it's not the idea that's important, as you don't have to discover something unique; it's really about how you do it. It's all about the execution, and that is something I can teach you.

THIS BOOK WILL...

This book will change the way you think about running a business and debunk the myths that suggest it is difficult.

When you finish reading it, you will have developed a clear plan about what you want your business to become, and defined a timeframe to achieve those goals.

If you are considering setting up on your own, it will show you the way to start, scale and sell the business.

It will also challenge you to think about the team you'll need to help you and the rewards you should give them.

CONTENTS

WHO THE HELL IS GARY ASHWORTH?

Gary is a serial entrepreneur who has bought, sold, started and scaled businesses in different sectors since he started his first company aged 21.

Some have gone on to win awards, such as the *Sunday Times' Best Small Companies to Work For*. Bigger ones have floated on the stock market; one was the fastest growing company on the list, which he went on to sell for 10 times the float price.

Some have failed, but they're the ones he learned the most from.

He's learned how to drastically increase the odds of success by constantly outpacing competitors and reminding owners of the end goals, while chunking waypoints down into bite-sized pieces.

He also embraces the arts. He's an award-winning theatre producer and has managed a comedian and a jazz singer, producing albums for both.

Gary genuinely believes the arts and commerce have more in common than most people realise. He thinks creative people need to learn to be more commercial, and businesspeople should learn to be more artistic.

He champions people, urges them to set high goals, holds them to account and coaches them from the sidelines to achieve them.

He still works as an investor, a coach, a cheerleader for start-ups and a non-executive director or chairman for a portfolio of businesses.

Gary likes to hear about success stories. You can contact him via his website at: **www.garyashworth.com/contact**

The chapters in this book are dedicated

to Oli, Char and Harrison.

Three entrepreneurs in the making.

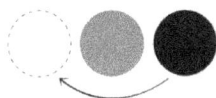

MY STORY

A low point of my life was when I was 16 and kicked out of school.

It was a good school too. An obsessively academic school, though, where the sharp wit and famous repartee I had relied on for survival at previous schools counted not one jot.

In a combination of disappointment and deep frustration, without realising what he was saying or doing, my father gave me the most motivating speech I've ever had in my life. I couldn't have been jolted into action more rapidly if I had been jabbed with a cattle prod, and his words still ring clearly in my ears today:

"WE'LL ALWAYS LOVE YOU, SON, EVEN THOUGH YOU'LL NEVER AMOUNT TO ANYTHING."

That was the switch I needed to change my life. In my angry head, I vowed to show him what I was capable of. I wish I'd realised at the time that the right path for me didn't involve working for anyone else. It took me four more years of experimenting with different jobs before I set up my own business.

I wish I'd known at the time that I should have focused on doing more of what I was good at instead of beating myself up for failing to live up to the norms that society brainwashes you into as a teenager.

I had passed an entrance exam and been accepted into a grammar school that had a great reputation as a sausage factory, churning boys out to trot off eagerly to Oxford or Cambridge and become lawyers, doctors, academics or similar. If you excelled at sports, that helped at the interview, too.

It wasn't for me. I made good friends at school, but the place was strict and steeped in tradition. It was an all-boys school with a compulsory uniform policy and a hierarchy of older boys, prefects, masters and tests. I was a 'day boy', meaning I got to go home at night, but many of my friends were boarders who lived at one or other of the school's boarding houses. We still had an ancient custom where the younger boys would take turns serving other boys' lunches and clearing up the dishes after them. It was quite a brutal school; lots of bullying and violence from both teachers and fellow students.

One of the teachers was famous for pulling prepubescent boys out of the showers while they were naked and taking them into the games cupboard, where he closed the door, made them bend over and gave them 'six of the best' whacks on their bare backside with a training shoe. In those days it was called 'discipline' and considered part of school life. Looking back, it was just child abuse.

I hated it. It taught me a healthy disrespect for authority. I began to question everything I was told; I still do. It was the making of me. I couldn't wait to leave.

STEPPING INTO ENTREPRENEURSHIP

I soon set about conjuring up plans to make money; I'd never been frightened of hard work. Being successful in these little enterprises gave me a sense of security I hadn't experienced in life until that time.

At 16, I organised a pop concert in our local town – there wasn't much else to do. I booked the venue and the bands, rented the music system. I printed posters and tickets, creeping back into school at night and using the art room printing press. I poured cups of soft drinks and sold them during the interval.

We sold out to capacity (the 300 tickets we had printed) in advance, but when more people arrived on the night, eager to get in, we sold some of the ticket stubs we had collected again and again. It was a success, and I made enough to buy my first car. If only all ventures were that easy.

Over the next four or five years, there were two permanent jobs and a few more hare-brained money-making schemes. After I'd slogged away for hours, month after month and for various employers, like a willing donkey, it didn't take me long to realise that I wasn't going to get rich working for somebody else. There was a higher risk of failure if I started my own business – but an uncapped reward. The lessons in this book will show you that you can reduce the risk of failure down to a manageable level without compromising the upside potential when starting a business.

At age 21, I set up my own accountancy recruitment business, which I went on to float on the London Stock Exchange and eventually sold for 10 times the float price. That's where I first started to learn how to scale businesses.

At age 22, I persuaded a bank to loan me enough money to mortgage a five-storey house in central London. It was full of Australians and New Zealanders working and travelling in Europe on working holiday visas. The location and flexibility suited them and the rent they paid suited me. It covered the monthly mortgage payments. That's where I learned the difference between good debt and bad debt when borrowing money.

At age 32, I produced my first play: *Wasp*, written by Steve Martin. That's when I learned how many similarities there are between the arts and business, and how ideas can cross over.

At age 34, I produced a jazz album for Rebecca Wheatley, someone I had met singing in Soho. I had no idea what I was doing. All I knew was that she could sing better than anyone I had ever heard, and I wanted a bigger audience to hear her. I was right; years later, despite my attempts to help, her career took off through her own hard work. The year 2020 saw her sing with Bryn Terfel to 12,000 people in the Albert Hall.

At age 39, I co-produced a show called *Anonymous Society*, which won the Total Theatre Award for best overall production at the Edinburgh Festival. I'd seen the show in a much bigger format in Antwerp, where two geniuses, Andrew Wale and Perrin Allen, had made a big impression; they arranged the music, directed the show, cast unique performers and created a surreal set in a shipyard that used to employ 5,000 workers.

I learned that the techniques used to build a company, stage a musical or produce an album are very similar. They require the assembly of passionate teams who all share the same dogged determination.

EXPECTATIONS AND FAILURES

I was adopted at six weeks old into a loving family but, although my childhood was happy, I suspect there was a lingering insecurity that has driven me to provide for myself and not be at the mercy or whim of others who may, quite rightly, have their own agendas.

I mentioned my father earlier. Although Keith and I got on famously, and I know he was very proud of me after I had become established, I did feel like I was a constant source of disappointment to him when I was growing up.

After he and my mother found out they couldn't have children, they adopted me and my sister and had high ambitions for us, perhaps unrealistic ones. My father hoped I'd either be Prime

Minister or the opening batsman for Lancashire. I wasn't that boy. I wasn't academic or sporty enough to rise to that level. He had an old-fashioned sense of logic, sticking to the rules and his sense of what was right and wrong. He had a terrific work ethic, which has rubbed off on me.

I remember a few years ago, watching a crime documentary on TV with him. A killer, Christopher Campano, had been found guilty of the first-degree manslaughter of his wife in 1992 and sentenced to 1,000 years in prison. My father looked at me, shook his head and said, without a trace of a smile, 'The justice system isn't what it used to be. He'll only serve half that time nowadays, you know.'

It's funny what drives people on. I wonder what would have happened if he'd died before I achieved success? I suspect I would have made myself unhappy by constantly trying to fulfil the impossible task of making a man who didn't exist any more proud of me.

Not all my businesses have been a success. I've had one or two disasters and some mediocre returns on my investment. I've backed the wrong people, been defrauded, got my timing wrong, been under-capitalised and not had the courage to pour good money after bad.

These painful lessons have been where I've learned the most. Like most people, I remember pain more vividly than pleasure and I've learned not to make the same mistake twice. In this book I've laid out my mistakes in all their agony, and the consequences of them too, so that you won't make them in the first place.

Running your own business isn't a dark art. It's something that can be learned. Some people in business pretend it's difficult because they don't want the competition. The reality is that there's a structure that can be learned – in fact, there's a set of principles that I lay out in this book to explain how to do it.

Selling products or services is more sophisticated nowadays, and it doesn't have to rely on dishonest strong-arm selling techniques. Motivating salespeople has moved on since the play *Glengarry Glen Ross*, where the first prize in the sales contest is a Cadillac Eldorado, the second prize is a set of steak knives, and the third prize is… you're fired!

Successful businesses win because their clients win too. It shouldn't ever be win/lose. Strong-arm sales techniques have been replaced with a deeper understanding of client challenges and finding ways to help solve them.

FINANCIAL SECURITY FOR LIFE

I now work as a coach, a non-executive director and an investor for passionate companies that are going places.

If in five years' time, I can look back and still be in contact with a growing community – those inspired to take the plunge and start their own businesses as a result of something they read within these pages, existing business owners who have learned how to aim high and chunk down the journey, or even people who merely downloaded the business growth template from my website and applied it – then the time I've spent writing this book will have been worthwhile.

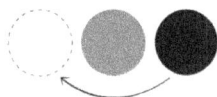

EAT THE
PUDDING FIRST

"IF YOU DON'T KNOW WHERE
YOU'RE GOING, ANY ROAD WILL
TAKE YOU THERE."

Lewis Carroll

WHAT IS EATING THE PUDDING FIRST?

I always set out my goals and work backwards from the end. I chunk down the milestones into bite-sized pieces, work out who's going to help me, then celebrate each milestone along the way until I reach my destination. And it works. It acts as a growth accelerator and reduces the time before you achieve your goals and sell.

I've used this technique over and over again for more than 20 years in different types of businesses, most recently having sold the majority share of an award-winning consulting business for cash. I'm currently helping a rapidly growing business in the healthcare sector and another one in talent management. In all cases, the management teams and I have a valuable chunk of ownership which we will all benefit from.

I deliberately surround myself with a team of people who will be part of the review mechanism, who assertively remind me of the endgame when I wander off course. After all, everyone wanders off course at times!

It's the same technique whether I'm starting a business, scaling up, or grooming one for sale. Successful people I have met always begin with the end in mind.

I gave the book this title because starting and running a business is a lot like eating a meal; there's a beginning, a middle and an end. Generally, they all have different flavours and provide different experiences, from the starter and the main course through to the dessert.

I love desserts! They might be strawberries oozing with cream, caramelised tarts or chocolate puddings. However, too often, by the time the menu comes, I'm either full or I've run out of time.

The business lifecycle is similar. Starting a business has a different flavour than scaling one up and requires very different skills,

"

WE SPEND OUR LIVES FOCUSING

ON WHAT'S URGENT AND FORGET

WHAT'S IMPORTANT.

"

beliefs and support systems. Selling a business, when the time is right, is a different process altogether.

WHY YOU NEED TO KEEP THE PUDDING IN MIND FROM THE BEGINNING

We all get blown off course from time to time. We get bogged down in the weeds and focus on solving the issues of that day or that week, that particular customer problem or that particular supply chain issue. We lose sight of the end goal. We spend our lives focusing on what's urgent and forget what's important.

How many successful businesses, ones that would have changed the world or enriched communities, never got off the ground? How many businesses survive from year to year, bobbling along but never reaching their full potential? How many businesses never get sold, leaving the dreams of their owners unfulfilled?

If the owners had managed to keep the pudding in mind and plan around it, how different things could have been! Keeping a constant reminder of your end goals tattooed on your brain will up the odds of success.

In this book, I try to remind us all of the reasons we took the risks and made the sacrifices we did to set up in the first place, because we need to focus on the outcome of our dreams. There are hundreds of distractions, wrong turnings and things that don't work that mean we end up getting beaten up by life itself. I want to act as your inner conscience that keeps you tenaciously trudging on, step by step, giving you the nourishment you need until you get to the finishing line!

Nailing down a business plan that works backwards from a sale to the present day produces a very clear path to follow and identifies the imperative mile-markers along the way, so that resources can be anticipated ahead of time. It can sometimes be counterintuitive to work backwards, which is why I've put together a series of questions that will help you do just this. It will also raise some points of consideration and guide the conversations you need to have (as well as outline who you need to have them with). It is something I wish I had years ago when I started out! You can grab that at **www.garyashworth.com/eatthepuddingfirst**

THE STAGES OF BUSINESS GROWTH

This book discusses each of the three stages of the business growth cycle in detail and sets out a formula for each section.

One of the chapters mentions Walt Disney. He's perhaps the man with the greatest imagination of our time, yet people who knew him said there were three very different Walt personality types, and they never knew which one was coming to the meeting. He could be a dreamer, a realist or a critic, and it's easy to link his success with the obsessive focus he had on each of these phases, to the exclusion of the others. He refused to let any foreign thoughts bleed into the mode he was working in at that time.

The lifecycle of most businesses is a similar three-way process, which is why we have broken the chapters into the three sections: start, scale and sell.

I'm not an academic, and I'm not a teacher. I'm an entrepreneur. A businessman who, over the years, has crafted techniques that work. I've learned the things that don't work too, and I have managed to cut my way through the noise, administration and crap that stops so many people progressing, like my excited labrador trying to swim through thick wet mud. All of the chapters are drawn from my own personal experience at the coal face.

I have written this book for two groups of people who could benefit from eating the pudding first:

1. Curious individuals who haven't taken the plunge yet – you know who you are! You've been wondering for a while now what it might be like to be responsible for your own destiny and have a share of the rewards it brings. It's my job to help take some of the risk out of your plan and tip you over the edge.

2. Existing business owners who want to turbocharge the growth of their business and reach their goals more quickly and elegantly. Having created your own business, you already have the skill and work ethic to succeed. My goal is to provoke you into aiming higher and achieving exponentially more in the same timeframe, without flogging yourself to death.

Be careful what you wish for. I'm hoping that your decision to purchase this book will be the start of something much more exciting, enriching and life changing!

It doesn't just work with business goals. It's common sense. Many groups of people successfully use the same strategy to conquer personal challenges too.

Last year, I found that my own weight had crept up over the years, to the point where I couldn't tie my shoelaces without holding my breath. I'd started to avoid mirrors and was getting fed up with being asked to dress up as Santa every December.

I adopted the same strategy I would do in business: I set the end goal first. Chunked it down into bite-sized smaller goals, then surrounded myself with a support team to succeed – personal trainers, nutritionists, slimming groups – and I wrote a routine that was very similar to a business plan. The result is that I am now 60 pounds lighter. I've bought a new wardrobe of clothes and feel a lot healthier. It's never easy, but it's always worth it.

It never starts with a plan, though; it starts earlier than that. It starts with the belief that you can succeed, and the desire and commitment to do it.

"THE GREATEST SIN YOU CAN EVER COMMIT TO YOURSELF IS TO WASTE YOUR LIFE WAITING FOR SOMEONE ELSE TO GIVE YOU MONEY."

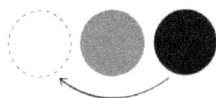

INTRODUCTION

I wrote this book because I believe success in business is something that can be both conveyed and learned. It doesn't take a particularly impressive skill set in order to achieve this; anyone with a degree of determination can do it.

I wouldn't claim to have any particularly outstanding abilities, but I've learned how to be successful and so now I want to share what I've gleaned along the way.

In this book, I set out the recipe for success, explaining the techniques and strategies that work in the world of business. It's not one unending procession of success stories, though; I've made my fair share of mistakes, and these are outlined in the text as well. I've proudly worn the scars of failure so that you can avoid them.

The reason I've named the book *Eat the Pudding First* is as a reminder for us all to begin with the end goal and work backwards.

Starting, growing and selling businesses is a great achievement. Watching a brand come to life, growing from the germ of an idea to a household name, gives you a tremendous sense of pride and satisfaction. It may not be as clever as painting a Rembrandt, but it is art nevertheless – hence my thoughts on the important crossover between the creativity of the arts and the pragmaticism of establishing a business. Hiring, growing and developing a workforce who are proud of what they do is also a skill in itself.

A week before I finished the book, I heard that one of the businesses I chair had been included in the *Sunday Times Top 100 Small Companies to Work For* and another will be included in the *Sunday Times Virgin Atlantic Fast Track 100* league table, which ranks Britain's top 100 private companies with the fastest growing sales over their latest three years, if they hit their budget for the rest of the year. The sense of achievement from those acknowledgements means as much or more to me than the profits the businesses themselves make.

The press and those not involved in business like to paint a picture of the horrors of business; they suggest that commerce is a filthy, cut-throat business, full of corruption and fraud, where people will stick a knife in you for a quid. That is not my experience. Of course, there are rotten apples in every barrel, and I have been duped and defrauded on occasion, but in the main I've met honest passionate men and women who care about their products, services and people.

It's not like competitive sport where one side wins and the other side loses. Where there's a willing seller and a willing buyer, everybody wins.

There are many topics covered within these pages that will provide the reader with a brief insight into the subject matter. I don't want this to be a definitive guide, or to discuss issues in exhaustive depth. What I have included is enough to make the most important points and to give you a grounding in business success.

If you do wish to delve into any of the topics in inordinate detail, there are books listed in the appendix that cover the material in far more depth.

I want to emphasise right now that I'm not an academic. I don't consider myself to be an intellectual. I'm a businessman, a successful self-taught entrepreneur, an adventurer, a bon viveur.

However, I'm also not scared of hard work or getting my hands dirty. I achieved my success in business the hard way. My sister and I were adopted at the age of just six weeks by loving and caring parents of old-fashioned northern stock. I wasn't educated at Eton, Oxford, Cambridge or Harvard. I had no particular aptitude nor fondness for school and was asked to leave my local grammar school at the age of 16, after failing to study sufficiently and being generally disruptive.

Funnily enough, I now live in a 400-year-old house that was built by the Borlase family – the people who built the very school from which I was unceremoniously ejected. I will forever recall the coat of arms that I used to have to wear on my blazer every day, with its pretentious Latin motto *Te Digna Sequere* (follow things worthy of thyself), and which was also permanently carved into one of the wood panels in the library.

This is a constant reminder to me of how our education system fails people like me, who are curious, have an unquestionable thirst to challenge silly rules and possess an old-fashioned, healthy disrespect for authority. But that's a different book! What I will say is that when you examine the careers of successful entrepreneurs, so many of them had a disappointing, difficult or derisory relationship with education.

Nonetheless, when I dropped out of school at the age of 16, with few qualifications or ideas on my future direction, my father gave me the most motivating talk of my life. The words that he said to me have never left me: 'We'll always love you, son, even though you'll never amount to anything.'

I had my fair share of menial employment when I was working out which businesses I would really throw my weight behind in the future. Telephone sales, van driver, commission-only door-to-door salesman… these were the sort of strictly unglamorous roles I resorted to in order to pay my rent. But when I organised that concert, aged 15, and earned enough to buy a car, I had tasted the feeling of being an entrepreneur. I soon became addicted to the concept of being responsible for my own destiny. I was never going to wait in line for a career path to escalate, or to be a slave to a barely adequate (and often inadequate) pay packet.

If you work hard and believe in yourself, at a certain point you will inevitably be handed an opportunity. Mine was to have the chance to work for a recruitment company, who trained me well and gave me a valuable insight into the world of commerce. My life was about to change forever.

The Conservative government of the day, headed by Margaret Thatcher, introduced a policy called the Small Firm Loan Guarantee Scheme. As part of this scheme, they would guarantee 80% of the debt that the bank lent companies, way outside of the risk guidelines of the time. It was a shrewd policy, intended to encourage people to begin businesses.

Another big plus point was that computerised records simply didn't exist at this time. As decisions were taken locally, this meant you could continue sending your business plan to multiple branches of all the banks until you finally located one that you could convince to give you an opportunity. This was my first lesson in cunning and persistence. The first four banks I approached turned me down, but the fifth – merely a different office of the same bank that had previously rejected me – eventually answered in the affirmative.

Fortune favours the persistent. My plan worked. I began my first legitimate company at the age of 21 and I've never taken a backwards glance since.

Over time, and with a huge amount of hard work invested in the process, my success steadily grew. Since then, I've travelled in private jets and owned super-yachts, exotic cars and property all over the world. I've floated businesses on the stock market along the way too. Still, please don't harbour the misapprehension that it's all been glamorous. I've also had bailiffs knock at my door, bought businesses that have gone bust and have lost vast amounts of money at times.

I've acquired a huge amount of knowledge and experience, but the greatest gift this journey has given me is the realisation that our capabilities and opportunities in life are limited only by the barriers we create for ourselves.

I'm still learning, and I hope that you learn from this book too.

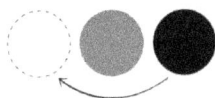

START

"THE SECRET TO GETTING AHEAD
IS GETTING STARTED."

Mark Twain

Don't wait too long to set up your own business, or you'll never get around to doing it. You'll think of all the reasons not to and chicken out. As soon as you have a robust business plan and you have tested the market, jump in with both feet – the water isn't as cold as you imagine, and the rewards can be unlimited.

The tips and tricks contained within the chapters in the 'Start' section of this book can dramatically help boost your chances of success and minimise the odds of failure when you're starting a business for the first time. However, it stands to reason that the more you have to lose, the greater the risk.

I always ask myself, 'What's the worst that can happen if it goes wrong?'

If you're slightly older, earning a fortune working for someone else whilst funding an extravagant partner with three kids at private school, along with the associated violin lessons, gym membership, Pilates classes, exotic holidays, eye-watering mortgage and vintage wine habit, then clearly that's a lot to walk away from.

At the other end of the spectrum, if you've dropped out of college to start a new crypto-currency business with a couple of mates in the basement of your rented accommodation, then it will be much easier to pick yourself up, dust yourself down and get a job with someone else if it all goes wrong. You've lost very little apart from a couple of ounces of pride and a small amount of time – which you'd have probably spent watching Netflix or gaming, anyway.

Most of us contemplating working for ourselves for the first time are somewhere in between these two extremes and can justify and even embrace the risk of failure. There's no doubt that a tiny amount of fear, some butterflies in the pit of your stomach, is a good thing, but the longer you leave it, the more comfortable your life may become and the more you'll have to lose. Waiting too long may cause the pendulum to swing too far away from you.

Don't get hung up on that unique idea that no one has thought of before. There are very few of them and, even if you are lucky enough to have invented a new type of power-free lightbulb, brand new concepts carry the highest risk of failure.

It's much better to choose something you have some knowledge of and feel passionate about. After all, ideas are overrated – it's all about execution and doing things better than your competitors. I've been involved with many start-ups and there are common challenges, but there are also things you can anticipate to better set yourself up for success.

I set up my first business when I was 21, in a room above a pub in the City of London. It was the prestige of the address that was important to me, not the luxury of the accommodation, because most of the work was done on the phone or by mail, and clients were met in coffee shops and hotel lobbies.

'Fake it till you make it,' was my motto.

It was an accountancy recruitment business. Since I'd made money doing the same thing working for someone else the year before, I thought I'd give it a go. I had become good friends with one of the interim accountants I had placed in a job, and he diligently helped me write the business plan as a favour.

On my first day, when the flat-pack desks arrived, I faced the stark realisation that no one was going to come and assemble them for me, and so I'd better get on with it. I also realised that if I just was capable of what I'd been doing when I worked for someone else, I'd be fine and soon get to the all-important break-even hurdle.

You will naturally feel vulnerable and slightly lonely at the beginning, not having the support systems around you that you might have taken for granted in full employment, which is why we spend time discussing the team you must assemble around yourself to fill those gaps. Feeling vulnerable isn't a reason to start with someone else there to keep you company, hold your hand and take half your equity too. If you feel lonely, get a dog or a cat instead!

Generally speaking (though not in all cases), the first year or two in business will involve a lot of scrimping and saving, looking after the pennies, bootstrapping your business, keeping all of the ownership yourself and borrowing money in the early days from friends, family and fools to fund the start-up losses.

I remember approaching my father with an ambitious but well-put-together business plan. I told him I needed to borrow £2,400, which even at that time wasn't a fortune. He read the plan thoroughly and told me that he didn't think it was a good idea.

In the end, I sold my car and paid the money into the bank account, proud to get started without his help. After months of hawking the plan to various financial institutions, the bank had agreed to fund the lion's share of the cash needed under the Small Firm Loan Guarantee Scheme, which was a brilliant government incentive to underwrite higher risk bank debt for start-ups at the time. I wondered whether they'd want to charge interest on the loan or insist on a small equity stake. They did neither.

I wasn't exactly sure I was doing the right thing at the time, but now I have the experience of starting many ventures, I'd do the same in a heartbeat. Every business I've started has had both pleasant and unpleasant surprises. It's all part of the journey. There's never been a smooth, steady journey from start to finish, but we learn to relish the challenges and luxuriate in the profits that are amassed by solving the problems. We all need to develop a slightly thicker skin to cope with the arrows that are thrown at us.

Eating the pudding first will make you stronger.

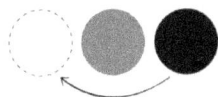

ANYONE CAN DO IT

"WHEN YOU BELIEVE THAT YOU CAN
DO SOMETHING, THAT'S WHEN YOU
CAN DO IT."

Joseph Gordon-Levitt

Success, intelligence and common sense don't necessarily go hand in hand. To be frank, there are some absolute idiots running successful businesses. You've probably encountered a few yourself. We bump into them regularly while going about our daily lives, shaking our heads in bewilderment at their incomprehensible ability to make a living. While this overall impression may be beguiling, it also points to a simple reality: if they can run successful businesses, why can't you?

Starting, running and maintaining a business may not be a life choice that everyone wishes to make, but it definitely shouldn't be viewed as a dark art either. There is no reason to be frightened about the prospect of launching a business; in fact, you have everything to gain from the process.

Another important aspect of starting a business that is often overlooked is that you don't need to chuck all your chips into the middle of the poker table immediately; in many cases, it's perfectly possible to keep going with your day job while you build the business based on your idea. Wait until your idea gains traction before you surrender your secure income. That's just common sense, right?

THE ILLUSION OF SECURITY

Jobs often offer the illusion of security, but it *is* an illusion. The days where a job was for life are resolutely over for most people; indeed, it's far more common to change positions and even careers on a regular basis. Companies frequently relocate operations overseas, downsizing, jettisoning unprofitable divisions and making all manner of other life-changing decisions in the blink of an eye. Even major companies liquidate on a fairly regular basis. There are no givens, no guarantees and no sure things in this highly competitive climate.

This even applies to civil service and government positions. It's becoming increasingly common for government departments to outsource parts of their operation, while positions in local government can be affected by wider political issues and manoeuvring. That's before we even consider the impact of robotics and the automation it will inevitably bring. It's already known that progress in this field will impact on millions of jobs all over the world. Prolific brains and family workers will be replaced by robots. It's already in the pipeline.

I don't mean for this to sound depressing, but it's just the reality. When confronted with the truth, we have two options: ignore it or face it. While it can be tempting to ignore unpalatable realities, this doesn't prevent them from being the case and, no matter how far we bend over and how deep we may bury our heads in the sand, the reality will still kick us up the backside!

SHIFTING CLIMATE

Responding to this shifting work climate is essential. I would argue that by investing in yourself and your own abilities, while developing your own skills and knowledge, you could be providing yourself and your family with a more secure future than by simply working for a weekly wage. Furthermore, you'll also be improving your own freedom and liberty at the same time.

Indeed, this is one of the primary reasons why people begin their own businesses in the first place. They want to be in charge of their own destinies and to surround themselves with close and like-minded people. Starting a business enables you to include family members and to have the opportunity to build something lasting, which can then be passed on to the next generation. The risks associated with building a business can be higher, and the workload can be significantly heftier, but the rewards are that much greater.

The other important thing to note is that there are hundreds, or possibly thousands, of types of businesses to choose from. We live in a hugely diverse culture and there are many commercial avenues now available to the budding entrepreneur. All you have to do is work out something that suits your particular skills and interests and pick up the baton.

IMPROVING OPERATIONS

Speaking of picking up the baton, another possible option for business owners is to purchase an existing business, then improve upon its operations. Franchising is another area that has proved popular with many entrepreneurs. Although the government can be criticised regarding some of its conduct towards business, and small and medium-sized enterprises in particular, there are avenues open to those looking to launch an enterprise. The UK government has attempted to support businesses with a variety of incentives, while tax-efficient loans are available for small businesses in most countries. Vendor financing can even be acquired in some cases – where the person you are buying from will allow you to pay the sale price over a period of time, sometimes even out of the profits you generate.

The Pareto principle, or the 80/20 rule, is something that applies across several areas of life, and running a business is no exception. When you're starting out with any commercial venture, you only rely on 20% inspiration, with the 80% perspiration making up the majority of your efforts. You cannot enter into this half-heartedly, or with anything less than total commitment. You must understand that your work–life balance will tip decidedly towards work for the first few years and that there will always be an element of risk involved in any business venture. But if you don't buy a ticket, you definitely won't win the raffle.

So, considering the level of commitment that is required to build a successful business, it is essential to ask yourself some important questions before beginning. I believe that central to this is simply focusing on what you would actually like to do best. Why remove yourself from one life sentence and then choose to commit yourself to another? The more passionate you feel about what you're selling, the more likely it is to be sold successfully.

Aside from this, it also makes logical sense to choose something at which you excel. You don't necessarily need to be the best; you just need to be better than most people. Try to assess your own skills objectively, work out your strengths and weaknesses, and then decipher how they correlate with possible business avenues. Be honest with yourself in both celebrating your strengths and candidly appraising your weaknesses.

I started my first business when I was 21 in a rented room above a pub called the Queen's Arms in the City of London. It was an accountancy recruitment business and the reason that I chose this is that I had already accrued some experience working for another company in a similar role. Choose what you know! On one level, it could have been viewed as daunting to launch the business at such a relatively tender age, but I viewed it as a massive advantage. I was a single guy, I didn't have a mortgage to pay, I had no family responsibilities. If I hadn't succeeded, there was absolutely nothing stopping me from picking myself up, dusting myself down and getting a nine-to-five job.

DON'T DIE WONDERING

However, there was one compelling factor that underpinned my decision to go into business. I didn't want to die wondering what would have happened if I had taken the chance. I didn't want to spend my working life ruminating on what would have happened if I'd only had the courage to start up by myself. Life is too short to live with regrets; they weigh far too heavily on you as you get older.

Nonetheless, don't labour under the misapprehension that I was some fearless d'Artagnan, gambolling merrily toward Paris! I definitely had my doubts, and I was certainly nervous about the process. It's completely natural, and even advantageous, to fully acknowledge the butterflies in the pit of your stomach. In fact, considering what you can do to mitigate against any fears that you might have is definitely a sensible policy.

In my situation, I decided to begin my business venture with an equal partner, which meant that I always had support. I started the business with a good friend, who I had worked with closely in my previous occupation. We both quit the job on the same day and began this exciting new venture together, in what we hoped would be heroic fashion!

Now here is another important aspect of business: don't be afraid to surround yourself with people more gifted than you. I acknowledge that my friend was more talented than me; I was the better salesman, but he had more attention to detail when it came to organising procedures, running the payroll and even conducting our accounts. Complementary skills are really important.

The trouble was that my business partner didn't enjoy the job of creating this new business. He found the repetitive nature of the work tedious and began to resent coming into work every day. On reflection, he hadn't properly considered the practicalities of building the business from scratch and running it during its infancy. After a bit of to-ing and fro-ing, we came to an amicable agreement, and I bought him out.

This went extremely well, and the company went from strength to strength. If we hadn't both been reasonable people, though, it could have ended in tears and thousands could have been squandered on legal fees working out the business divorce.

DO YOU NEED A PARTNER?

The thing to learn from this experience is that it's definitely worth considering having a business partner, but it is something that needs to be thought about diligently. Do you really need a business partner, or are you just looking for someone to hold your hand? Because if it's the latter, you haven't got yourself into the right mindset to succeed in business. It's definitely great to have support, but there needs to be a fiercely independent streak at the core of your soul. Building and running a business can get lonely; you have to rely on yourself to make the big decisions, and that requires a particularly single-minded outlook.

When I launched my first business, I believed I needed a partner who possessed complementary skills. However, after many years of experience, I now realise that skills can be bought in and that you don't need to surrender half of your equity in order to acquire them. Nowadays, I always ask the same three simple questions when I'm looking at setting up any business:

1. How much will it cost?

2. How much will it make?

3. How long will it take?

That normally cuts through the bluster, takes the emotion out of things and focuses the mind on what's really important.

However, it's also vital to be aware of your financial resources. Setting up a business often takes longer and costs more money than you initially believe, so it's better to overestimate the investment you will need to make. The first question I ask myself before embarking on any venture is, 'If it costs twice as much and takes three times as long to reach profitability as I expect, will I still be happy with the type of money that I've spent?' It's only if I'm able to answer yes to this question that I will give the project the green light.

UNREALISTIC TIME PERIODS

I'm keen to emphasise that there is seldom such a thing as an unachievable goal, but unrealistic time periods are all too common. Businesses need time to nurture, much like an attentive gardener tending to a bonsai tree. You have to factor in this reality when launching any business, as your idea will inevitably need structure, goals and strong financial control.

But you don't need to decide on your path before beginning the business. If you don't know where you're going, any road will take you to your destination. I'm a big fan of writing down a business plan, usually covering a three-year period, which provides a blueprint and journey map for you to follow throughout the adventure. On top of this, I would recommend implementing a structured review mechanism, which takes the form of a monthly board meeting. During this important assessment mechanism, you can examine and review sales versus budget, management accounts and cash flow.

I meet people working in business all the time who have lost sight of the profitability and potential of the companies they own. They get up to work really hard on these ventures every day and yet they've forgotten the reason they got into business in the first place. Some are in denial about their poor level of profitability, rushing around like busy fools.

However, no matter how hard you are working, it is absolutely essential to stay ahead of the curve and understand precisely where your business stands in the bigger picture. Many huge companies have folded because they failed to move with the times. Blockbuster Video had 60,000 employees, 9,000 stores worldwide and a value of $5bn in its prime, but it still failed and liquidated. Businesses can go past their sell-by date, just like mouldy sausages in a refrigerator.

Furthermore, it's not just your business that needs to evolve regularly; people need to change and grow as well. I often encounter people working in business who proclaim that they have been doing that particular job for 30 years. In reality, this isn't strictly accurate; they often actually did the job for one year and then repeated the experience a further 29 times. If you don't learn from your experiences, you will never evolve, the grass will grow under your feet and your business could then become completely untenable, like Blockbuster, Kodak, Blackberry, Polaroid and all the others.

RIDING A DEAD HORSE

Finally, there are times when things just don't work out for businesses, no matter how much energy you have invested in them. If you find yourself in this situation, it's vital to recognise the reality. You don't want to be throwing good money after bad, jettisoning cash into an unending black hole. It's commonplace to become hugely emotionally invested in a business, and sometimes it's difficult to see the wood for the trees. We think, because of the hours and sweat that we've put into a particular venture, that it simply has to be a success and so we tell ourselves that the problems can still be fixed if we work even harder. Unfortunately, this is a total delusion; ultimately, a faulty business model simply can't be fixed.

It's at times like these that it is vital to consult someone external, someone who's emotionally disconnected from the vast effort that you have invested into the business. You need someone with extensive business knowledge and experience to take a chilly and unemotional look at your company and offer you advice on its viability. Even if you've done everything right and created a valuable enterprise, that doesn't mean it will necessarily last forever. Only 10% of the original Fortune 500 companies that were listed in 1955 remained on the list in 2020.

If you're riding a dead horse, don't flog it – the horse won't appreciate it and you'll just make a spectacle of yourself! Get off and move on.

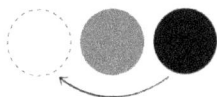

AIM HIGH

"AIM HIGH. YOU MAY STILL MISS THE
TARGET, BUT AT LEAST YOU WON'T
SHOOT YOUR FOOT OFF."

Lois McMaster Bujold

Where's *your* private jet?

You haven't got one, have you? And the reason for that is that you haven't aimed high enough. You haven't set goals that scare you, because you're frightened that you might not achieve them. Instead, you've opted for something more pragmatic: building up slowly and working towards your loftier ambitions.

Well, you're wrong. You should set them, and you can achieve them.

I've learned over the years that there is seldom such a thing as an unachievable goal – just an unachievable timeframe. Yes, getting to where you want to be might take slightly longer than you may wish, but I can assure you that even the most challenging goals are not impossible – unless you don't aim for them in the first place!

STARTING PRINCIPLES

Getting to places that may seem unimaginable begins with some simple principles. Aiming high is the first step towards achieving them. We've all heard the expression 'Shoot for the moon. Even if you miss, you'll end up amongst the stars.' This was originally conjured up by American minister and author Norman Vincent Peale, but it has been used by all and sundry. It may be a cliché, but it still makes perfect sense.

Getting yourself in the right mindset for your journey is also important, so make sure you give yourself a HUG – a High Goal – before you begin. Then you can start at the end of your journey and work backwards. Work out where you really want to be and then split the journey into bite-sized pieces that can be digested easily.

Ambitious goals shouldn't be intimidating, but they should make you slightly nervous. The sensation should be similar to when a great concert pianist goes out to perform, or the feelings top sportsmen and women experience before a huge encounter. You get butterflies, you get a nervous feeling in the pit of your stomach… and that is exactly how you're supposed to feel when you're pursuing something worthwhile.

STANDING OUT

If lofty goals were simple to accomplish, everyone would achieve them, and it would be considerably more difficult to punch through and stand out from the crowd. Just by aiming high in the first place, you're really standing out from the rank and file, and this immediately gives you every chance of success.

Writing your plans down in detail is a crucial first part of the process, ensuring that you know all of the waypoints on the path to your goal. That's the preparation. As soon as you're ready to go, you should then press the pedal to the metal and hold on tight.

You're now going to have to work hard until you get there. Work– life balance will be a term that is conspicuous by its absence from your vocabulary. There will be nothing but extremely long hours for quite some time, but that's the commitment required in order to get to the top of the mountain. The peak isn't easy to scale, but it is achievable if you make the appropriate preparations and truly buy into the journey. Indeed, while we're on the subject of mountains, those who scale Everest and reach other peaks are often driven by the single-minded attitude of: 'Someone's going to be first and it's going to be me.'

Another critical piece of advice that I would offer is to choose something that you enjoy doing. This applies across all fields.

Every single person I have encountered who has achieved excellence in any field has absolutely loved what they have chosen. This is what is required to put in the work in the first place, to push through the inevitable barriers and obstacles you encounter along the way and to still love the process at the end of it. When you find that thing in your life, you can almost rest assured that you're going to achieve success. Who was it who said that if you love what you're doing, you'll never work a day in your life?

ENJOY THE JOURNEY

So make sure that you really enjoy what you choose, because you are going to be spending a lot of time with yourself during this journey. If you cannot enjoy it and smell the roses along the way, you will face a pretty miserable experience, which will ultimately be unfulfilling no matter how successful you are, hampering your journey.

Speaking of which, it is imperative to begin with the end of your journey in mind. When you set off on a car journey, you begin by typing the destination into the satnav and then you follow directions and waypoints to plot your route. Effectively, you work backwards nowadays when you're driving a car to a distant location; you certainly don't just get in and start driving randomly (like some Uber drivers I've met).

The same principle applies in business. You must define your end goal and be able to see the endgame, much as a talented chess player will think many moves ahead, spotting long-term weaknesses in their opponent's position. They know they're going to checkmate the opposition king well before the end of the game, just as you should be able to see where you're going in business long before you arrive.

ENJOY THE VIEW

When you do achieve your goal, buy your jet, move in to your dream house, or even make enough money to get divorced, make sure you stop for a while, pat yourself on the back and enjoy the view. Remember where you've come from and appreciate how far you've travelled. Don't allow yourself to be constantly pounding the treadmill. As Ferris Bueller said in the movie bearing his name: 'Life moves pretty fast. If you don't stop and look around once in a while, you could miss it.'

Make sure you share your success with other people as well. It might sound glamorous, but there's nothing worse than flying on a private jet by yourself, even if you do know where you're going.

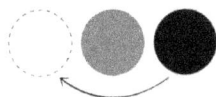

SPECIALISE OR RISK FAILURE

"THE SHOEMAKER MAKES A GOOD SHOE
BECAUSE HE MAKES NOTHING ELSE."

Ralph Waldo Emerson

The science fiction writer Robert Heinlein was considered a renaissance man. His philosophy of life recommended that:

"A HUMAN BEING SHOULD BE ABLE TO
CHANGE A DIAPER, PLAN AN INVASION,
BUTCHER A HOG, CONN A SHIP, DESIGN
A BUILDING, WRITE A SONNET, BALANCE
ACCOUNTS, BUILD A WALL, SET A BONE,

COMFORT THE DYING, TAKE ORDERS, GIVE ORDERS, COOPERATE, ACT ALONE, SOLVE EQUATIONS, ANALYSE A NEW PROBLEM, PITCH MANURE, PROGRAM A COMPUTER, COOK A TASTY MEAL, FIGHT EFFICIENTLY, DIE GALLANTLY. SPECIALISATION IS FOR INSECTS."

He was talking crap.

It's a lovely thought from a writer of fiction, but in business it is complete fantasy and ultimately makes no commercial sense.

The most successful people in a wide range of fields are specialists in their particular skill sets. That is, indeed, how they master what they do. This is why the '10,000 hours of practice for mastery' theory was authored; getting seriously good at something requires an enormous amount of commitment.

With this in mind, it's better to be a trusted source of knowledge in your own niche – or, even better, the irresistible first choice in what you do. Your knowledge might only be an inch wide, but it's a mile deep. That way, you can charge premium prices for being the best in the business and anyone who's anyone will want to work with you.

Of course, it is reasonable to acknowledge that this isn't the only business model. There are companies known for piling things high and selling them cheap – Primark being perhaps the best UK example – and it's impossible to deny their success. Nonetheless, this is an extremely tough way to make a living, and corners often have to be cut in order to remain profitable. This frequently involves the use of cheap and unethical labour, with dubious operations being located in poorly paid jurisdictions known for their dismal working conditions. In these circumstances, the whole operation becomes rather dubious, and ultimately of nebulous value.

UNREWARDING EXISTENCE

Almost inevitably, deciding to be the cheapest option means a race to the bottom. You can't produce anything of real quality, as you're inherently focused on affordability. Considering that idea, before you decide your business strategy you will need to reflect on whether you would enjoy being hunched up in the corner, like a whipped dog, scrapping around in a low-margin business that barely breaks even. How would you feel about marching to the drum of well-trained purchasers who are just interested in acquiring whatever you're selling as cheaply as possible? Think about it: they are the people who have plenty of other options if you won't meet their demands...

My view is that this is an unrewarding existence. It's not likely to be a fulfilling career, and you're not exactly likely to become wealthy from pursuing this path. Even if you do hit upon a profitable niche with this approach, will you really get the same enjoyment and sense of fulfilment and achievement from it that you would from investing in something of real quality?

I can only tell you my perspective: I'd rather pick pennies out of poo – it's less humiliating. There aren't many multi-million-pound entrepreneurs playing this game. It's not impossible, but locating one is only slightly easier than finding a dodo egg.

SHIFTING ETHOS

I think there is a simple reason why this approach no longer reaps rewards. The whole ethos of retail has changed immeasurably in recent years. People have more disposable income and are constantly looking for quality experiences. How many of us want to go to the cheapest restaurant, buy the least expensive suit, or shop for the lowest-priced pair of shoes? This pile high, sell cheap mentality simply doesn't mesh with the attitude of the age.

So now we've established these basic principles, my advice is to specialise in a certain area. Be proud of having mastered what you do and be ready to charge slightly above average for a better product or service. That is the best way to build consistent value, attract repeat business and create satisfied customers.

If you're looking to succeed in this way, the position and brand of your company both become particularly important. Some online firms have achieved virtual monopolies and completely dominate the markets in which they operate. This can then lead to some incredibly high valuations for products and services, because profits roll in rapidly and repeatedly.

INTERNET BIG BOYS

We have certainly seen companies like this being established over the last couple of decades. The big internet power brokers have become hugely popular, achieving some level of domination, with Google, Apple and Facebook now household names all over the world. I read recently that Amazon has stopped advertising completely in some regions because there's no point; everybody knows who they are. Everybody already buys from them!

There are several advantages to specialisation. Focusing on your market niche can give you a better customer value proposition, meaning that you speak directly to your target market. It also narrows down the number of people who compete with you, naturally ensuring that you have a more prominent place in your niche. This then gives you a higher level of gravitas, and pretty soon you can even charge more for your services, because you're viewed as a recognised brand. Plus, if you're just concentrating on one area, you're likely to be at the cutting edge of new developments, trends and innovation, giving you another advantage over competitors.

Setting yourself apart from your competitors is always the way forward. It's always valuable to demonstrate that you are particularly skilled and competent in your field and that you're delivering something that isn't commonplace. When you're engaging in any business venture, I would recommend continually asking yourself the following two questions:

- How do I show the world that I'm an expert?

- How do I set myself apart from the competition?

SETTING YOURSELF APART

There are a variety of ways that you can achieve this, but I would say that visibility is key. It's all about making yourself stand out from the crowd and in the marketplace. Sponsoring events or awards can be one excellent way of achieving this, as you gain a form of niche advertising and associate yourself with excellence in Pavlovian fashion.

Another good opportunity is to run workshops for customers, asking them to provide feedback on your products and services. This becomes a two-way process; they observe that you are listening to them, while you gain insight from their critical opinions. Another similar option is to speak at trade events and conferences, although this will tend to elevate your image with competitors rather than customers.

Aside from this, content is king nowadays. You should make every effort to author as much content as possible, and this can take several forms. Producing surveys, white papers, thought leadership pieces, industry news, gossip, networking events and breakfast talks will all be valuable. Anything that places you at the heart of a particular industry and sets your company or brand up as an authority. There are so many innovative things being done with social media nowadays that it's imperative you should understand these potentially valuable platforms.

Marketing content

The most powerful way of standing out from the crowd has emphatically been to produce and distribute your own marketing content. This can be an excellent way of getting ahead of the competition while also advertising yourself to a potential client base.

The great thing about marketing content is that it doesn't need to be too long, complex or involved. It doesn't even need to be produced by a professional marketing consultant or firm. What your marketing content should be focused on is delivering authenticity – an incredibly valuable attribute in this digital age when everything can be faked and nothing is sacred. If you can really deliver something that engages your audience and marks you out as being an authentic and distinctive brand, it can be hugely valuable for your business. With a little bit of practice, you can write your own material internally as an alternative to an outside marketing or PR company, while still achieving the same level of traction.

Video content can be particularly effective, and isn't necessarily difficult to produce and add subtitles to. Recording short pieces to camera with a smartphone is straightforward and there is an obvious and easily accessible distribution pathway: you could use your company website, Facebook, LinkedIn, the ubiquitous YouTube, your customer list, trade publications and so on. Whatever you choose to do, you know that you have a potentially captive audience at your fingertips.

Achieving engagement

If you're going to go down this route, it is important to be prepared for the long haul; particularly when using social platforms, engagement is all about delivering regular content. You need to be publishing on a consistent basis – at least weekly, and possibly even daily. The more you engage with your audience, the more they will be interested in what you do and the more momentum you will provide for your social platforms and video content.

In terms of the actual material, articles that help your users understand your products, news items that benefit the community you are serving, and even personal content that shows you and your company to be human can be valuable. Ultimately, you want to deliver something of value to your audience, content they will review as interesting to watch, rather than a chore.

You also have to remember that cutting your teeth in this area can be challenging. Perception is everything, and you can't expect to engage vast numbers of people immediately. Achieving traction in online content takes time and you will have to keep plugging away, constantly measuring the position that you occupy in the market.

MAKING PROGRESS

It's also worth noting that the first time you provide a product or service, you are merely a rookie, an inexperienced novice in the game, but within a few months, you will have evolved into someone who understands the market and can deliver something more appropriately directed towards your target market. As your experience evolves further still and you're pumping out content on a regular basis with a sizeable audience, you have now developed into an industry spokesperson. In a matter of months, you become the irresistible first choice in your sector and now have all the eyes of the industry trained on your existence.

Three years ago, I invested in a City-based, generic banking recruitment business, buying out one of the partners who had lost interest in it. The company had been successful in the past, but was now barely profitable, servicing contract banking roles. Staff were jittery and earnings were declining. The overall picture wasn't positive, but we had a clear plan to revitalise it.

We changed the business model to specialise in compliance, risk and regulation, which saw an immediate turnaround in margins, profits and average monthly billings per consultant. Fresh talent found the new offering compelling and a culture of 'someone's going to be first, and it's going to be me' rapidly emerged. The business thrived and, just two short years later, the company was sold – at which point, the owner pocketed several million pounds.

It's not the early bird who gets the worm any longer – it's the content writer.

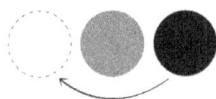

WHO'S HELPING
YOU START RIGHT?

**"ACCEPTING HELP DOESN'T MEAN
GIVING UP CONTROL."**

Sarah Dessen

Sometimes the outcome of a particular venture is unpredictable. I'm sure that virtually everyone reading this book has been part of a talented and enthusiastic team that surprisingly failed, or has been privileged enough to be part of a seemingly haphazard team that surprised everyone by succeeding, almost by accident.

However, although this latter scenario may seem to be random and unpredictable, nothing happens by chance. There is always an underlying cause and effect, a reason why things worked or didn't.

PREDICTING SUCCESS

Wouldn't it be great if we could better predict the likelihood of success before starting the project? If we could identify and understand the underlying factors that lead to success well before we began working? Well, I firmly believe that it's possible to tilt the odds of success distinctly in your favour. With practice, you can do this effectively by understanding the desirable composition of the ideal team.

When I say 'ideal', this is obviously different from 'perfect'. There is no such thing as the perfect team, so long as human beings are involved. However, you can still put together an extremely effective outfit while acknowledging the foibles associated with all of humanity.

I believe there are two fundamental factors which combine to create an effective team: the first is authentic diversity of thought, and the second is authentic diversity of skills. When these two qualities collide, they will effectively create a team that is more suited to specific tasks, covering all possible bases. It will be a flexible and multi-faceted group and one that almost inevitably achieves excellent results.

Putting together an authentic and successful team is all about balancing the people's qualities with their shortcomings. For example, we all know that individuals who excel in certain areas can often have equal and opposite traits that are unhelpful in group discussions. This doesn't mean that you should exclude these people, rather that you should utilise them effectively.

TEAM DYNAMICS

In attempting to understand the dynamics of teams, Meredith Belbin and Henley Management School defined eight balanced clusters of team roles that need to come together in order to ensure successful outcomes. This can be seen as rather similar to the Myers–Briggs personality test, which seeks to identify the identity of a person's character and behaviour.

As part of their research, they identified accurate methods for evaluating which categories individual members of staff sit in. Understanding these roles can be extremely valuable in building an effective team. The following information is my slight adaptation of their classification.

The implementer

This is a person who wants to get things done – an individual who isn't too concerned about technicalities and what they would deem to be tedious academic flotsam. They want to achieve practical things and follow processes through to their natural outcomes. Implementers are practical, systematic, loyal and come complete with a huge amount of common sense.

Conversely, implementers can be conservative in nature and might not be particularly tolerant of flighty, creative and artistic types. This doesn't apply across the board, but implementers are effectively pragmatists, who are more concerned with getting from A to B than discussing theoretical ideas at great length.

The coordinator

This is a calm, confident and controlled individual who is balanced in their approach to life and work. This person works extremely well in a team environment and can be relied upon to bring people together. Coordinators often automatically assume leadership roles and can be relied upon to play peacemaker in times of conflict.

Coordinators can always see the bigger picture and take care of both team members and the team as a whole. Coordinators understand the value of collaboration and want everyone to feel included. They're also ideal team players in an era of diversity, naturally communicating and relating to people from a wide variety of backgrounds. Coordinators help oil the wheels of commerce and ensure that teams tick over effectively.

The shaper

Shapers are extroverted, assertive and dynamic. They are the sort of charismatic people that tend to attract attention. Shapers want to be successful, they want their projects to be the best and they want to taste the trappings of winning!

Motivation is never a problem for anyone in the shaper category. These are highly self-motivated people, with a seemingly inexhaustible supply of energy. There is no problem too challenging for a shaper; they have an unquenchable desire to get things done, and crash through obstacles with ease. Shapers make ideal entrepreneurs and will drive the talented but lackadaisical members of a team through to successful delivery.

The plant

Plants are creative people. Of the eight groups of people, the plant is the most individualistic and arguably the most unusual. These are people who think outside the box and are never afraid to either challenge the status quo or appear heretic in their opinions. These people speak their minds and couldn't care less about the consequences!

If you can channel the skills and ability of plants, then you will have some exciting ideas on your hands. Often a member of this group will voice some concept that appears bizarre and unworkable, but which upon further inspection turns out to be brilliant. Never dismiss what the plant is saying, as it could end up making a huge amount of money, but do realise that these people need space and creative freedom.

The resource investigator

Resource investigators can be seen as another pragmatic and practical group within the structure of teams, and one that is particularly focused on understanding what resources are available. This group understands that seeing a project through to completion means making the most of the raw materials on offer and crafting them into the best products and services possible.

These are curious and enthusiastic people, who tend to bond extremely well with others. Resource investigators are always awake to new opportunities and always see the possibilities around them. When they feel that a project is important, they will always follow it through to the very end, offering practical and insightful suggestions along the way.

The monitor evaluator

This group has a calculating nature and can be relied upon to iron out all of the details of any important project. Monitor evaluators will drill down to the absolute brass tacks of an issue and engage in the most serious and careful checks imaginable. They make ideal auditors and can be an excellent counterpoint to some of the creative people in your organisation. Monitor evaluators will calm some of the less desirable aspects of plants and plants will encourage monitor evaluators to let down their hair occasionally!

If you're looking to make a decision on any business topic, monitor evaluators will carefully think through the consequences of these decisions and provide you with a thoughtful and diplomatic verdict. These are great people to have on your side if you're more of a big-picture than a details person.

The completer finisher

This group contains some of the most conscientious and detail-oriented people in any organisation. They are there to put the final coats of gloss on a particular project, seeing things through to the end and ensuring that the final product is up to the requisite standard.

The team worker

Finally, every good team needs its fair share of team workers. These are supportive, sociable and sensible people, who have the common touch and support the effectiveness of the whole team. Team workers are diligent in conducting their duties and work well as part of a collective. They are the glue of an organisation, the nuts and bolts that ensure things operate successfully at shop floor level.

Having a good mix of these eight groups leads to the ideal team. Not only will you have an excellent combination of skill sets, but you will also have a group of personalities that complement one another and provide balance to your company.

DIVERSITY OF THOUGHT

Speaking of balance, diversity of thought should be considered imperative in any company. If you're too stereotypical in your thinking and behaviour, you will fail to keep pace with your more forward-thinking and innovative competitors. Having a diverse workforce can really assist with problem-solving, as it will inevitably bring more creativity to the business. The greater the variety of perspectives you encounter, the more ideas you are likely to receive. This can only help the creative process.

Another obvious advantage of a mixed team is that you immediately reduce discrimination and create what will be an inclusive and modern workplace. You are encouraging a worldwide vision and ensuring that employees come into contact with a wide range of different opinions. This can only improve employee satisfaction and make your workplace a more interesting proposition for those who work there.

The great thing about diversity is that running a bigger business has become considerably more feasible. By using online marketing and other tools available on the internet, it's actually not difficult to run a global company from even the most obscure and remote location. You can draw together a virtual team with ease, and this team can then deliver results for you in the real world. Having a variety of different sources all providing inputs into the thinking process of the company will make it easier to understand the nuances of a broad range of customer needs. This will potentially broaden your appeal and ultimately increase revenue.

Unconscious bias

However, no matter how much we may be committed to diversity, none of us are completely objective. When engaging in any form of hiring, it's important to understand the degree of unconscious bias contained within all of us. No matter how hard we may try to remove any favour, we are all affected by our personal experiences and all of us are subjective in our assessments.

This can have a big impact on the way that we put teams together. From day one, when interviewing and selecting new staff members, we tend to choose traits and personalities we are familiar with and understand more readily. This makes perfect sense;

effectively, we are in a comfort zone. However, it is definitely not desirable. In fact, it can be debilitating, since this tendency can lead to us hiring the same types of people continually. This then in turn leads to restricted thinking, small-mindedness and pre-dictable decision-making.

Extra mile

Being aware of this issue isn't always enough to remedy it. We need to go the extra mile to incorporate this reality into the induction and training processes which help managers write job specifications, interview thoroughly and ultimately recruit effectively. We all need to fight for equality of opportunity every single day – a true meritocracy, where anyone can achieve any-thing they deserve. Equally, people should not be shamed into taking roles for which they are not ideally suited and which they don't even want in the first place.

Building a culture in which we make the most of the diverse talent pool available in our organisations is absolutely essential. This can be achieved by mentoring and coaching those who, for whatever reason, have not been given the same opportunities in their earlier career. It's imperative that we address this issue and ensure that these individuals who have been under-represented are instead provided with a clear path to reach their full poten-tial.

TRAINING GAINS

I know from my own experience, with a working career of over 40 years, that coaching and mentoring can make an astonishing difference to performance. When you have the right teacher, you can learn new skills that you would have believed impossible, and this collaborative process can really help boost the skills and self-belief of talented people.

Some years ago, I decided that I would like to learn to fly a helicopter. I signed up for several months of intensive training in the classroom, on the ground, and in the air in the actual aircraft. This eventually led to me passing my test and being let loose to fly solo in a specific type of helicopter. Just reading how to do it wouldn't have helped; I had to go up with an instructor, making the mistakes myself and learning exotic terms like *entering vortex ring state* or *overpitching*.

While it's nice to have the ability to do this, there is no doubt that it was the training that enabled me to reach this goal. If I had been left in the field with a helicopter, I would have had a serious accident, no matter how much time I spent experimenting. Coaching can strengthen the muscles our staff need to help them be the best possible versions of themselves. The same is true in business. You have to make mistakes to learn to do things properly, from your first sales call to your first day as CEO. There's an expression I like in the coaching community, that 'learning is only a rumour until you get it into the muscle.'

When you get a diverse mix of hungry, incentivised, well-trained people who are well led and focused on simple goals that are broken down into timeframes that seem challenging but achievable, then your staff will form an invincible army, one that will surprise you, smashing through obstacles with collective confidence and achieving almost any target you set them. It's quite a privilege to belong to that kind of group, and there's a tendency to get carried away with their pace and enthusiasm, where the initiative of the pack helps them to find their own solutions to the hurdles they encounter along the way.

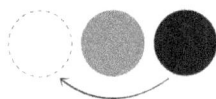

BUSINESS, CREATIVITY AND THE ARTS

"CREATIVITY IS ONE OF THE LAST REMAINING LEGAL WAYS OF GAINING AN UNFAIR ADVANTAGE OVER THE COMPETITION."

Ed McCabe

Business, creativity and the arts don't necessarily go together in the most natural manner. I'm sure most people think that the three things have absolutely nothing in common, but this superficial impression would be completely incorrect.

The ultimate aims and outcomes of these types of businesses might be significantly different, but the processes involved in creating something exciting, heart-warming and unique to the point of being mould-breaking have a great deal in common, and they often attract people with similar outlooks and passion.

THE HUMAN SPIRIT

It is part of the human spirit to imagine a better future. We humans are unique in imagining the future and asking questions. Animals don't do it in the same way. No labrador planned a trip to the moon, and you won't see a giraffe conducting an orchestra, yet humans from extremely diverse backgrounds invest a huge amount of time in foreseeing what will occur in the future.

Some particularly visionary individuals play a major role in shaping the future. Peter Drucker, the management consultant and philosopher, noted that 'the best way to predict the future is to create it.' Now there are nearly eight billion curious brains in this world, cogitating, considering, visualising what tomorrow could be like, the potential for human evolution has never been higher. When this natural human curiosity is allied with modern technology, the human race has the potential to reach extraordinary heights.

Many of these creative types are continually asking imaginative questions. What would happen if we do it this way instead? What would it be like if…? If only…

They have the imagination to envisage a different future – hopefully, a brighter one – and once something is imagined, we get very enthusiastic about experimenting with new ideas. When you consider this happening on a mass scale all over the planet, it's no wonder that changes are coming thick and fast in business, and that in the arts we stagger in hopeless bewilderment.

BUILDING A BETTER FUTURE

Ultimately, I would argue that business, creativity and the arts are united by the spirit of change and building a brighter future… creating something that will inspire people. It's a pioneering perspective that underpins the best examples in every field. Artists, actors, writers, musicians, entrepreneurs, all creative professionals, typically have one thing in common – the desire to create an imprint on the world and to change the way we look at things.

I'm not saying that artists and businesspeople are necessarily conjoined twins. Some might argue that the need to focus on the bottom line and earnings per share stifles artistry and that collaborations between the business community and the creative community represent 'selling out' because there's profit involved, but I disagree.

Even the most avant-garde projects require some boundaries; there is no such thing as completely unbridled creativity. Any form of art without structure and practical considerations will fall short of its ultimate intent. Meanwhile, business and entrepreneurial enterprises almost always require an injection of some of the creativity inherently associated with the arts.

TAKING RISKS

It seems to me that creativity, or at least the kind of creativity that you want to share, is about risk-taking within some type of structure that connects you with the present. If you're riding way ahead of the pack, it's important to turn around every now and again and make sure there's still someone following you. There is such a thing as being ahead of your time, and this is undoubtedly an accusation that has been levelled at projects in both the arts and business worlds. Sometimes it's great to be ahead of the curve, but most of us want to be noticed and appreciated in our own lifetimes. It seems a tragedy that so many cultural giants died penniless – Vincent Van Gogh, William Blake, Oscar Wilde and my grandad (in my opinion, anyway).

Another thing that unites both artists and business leaders is their embracing of risk-taking. This is something that entrepreneurs and creative people both relish; they are categorically not frightened of it. Indeed, they understand that it's an important component of succeeding in their particular fields. Sometimes it's necessary to push the envelope in the business world in order for a company to reach its true potential, while safe and staid artistic productions are less likely to win acclaim than those that challenge our assumptions and force us to view the world in a different way.

This propensity for risk means that both businesspeople and the creative community tend to see the future differently from the rest of the population. They have the foresight to see possible futures before they arise, and this can often unite the two apparently disparate communities, as businesspeople realise the benefits that collaborating with creative, artistic types can make to the overall operation. They ultimately see the involvement as an investment and not a cost.

I've been fortunate enough to work as an award-winning theatre producer and the manager of a jazz singer at the same time as working as an entrepreneur and the CEO of a public company. I have learned many life lessons from these disparate experiences.

NURTURING CREATIVITY

Firstly, the creative process can be nurtured. There is an ongoing debate about the difference between nature and nurture, about where the divide between natural talent and hard work begins and ends. There's an assumption that the creative arts require natural talent and inspiration that come from within or are sprinkled liberally on a person at birth.

While I wouldn't deny that some people are uniquely gifted, I believe that anyone can learn a form of creative proficiency – even the driest accountant! There is artistry in everything we do, including the way that we lead a team and how we make and execute our business plans. Creativity is positively hardwired into our collective DNA and has been part of the human experience for thousands of years.

It's also true that challenges and necessity often lead to solutions that wouldn't normally be possible, or at least would remain undiscovered. Creativity doesn't come from knowing the answer; it comes from *not* knowing the answer. Let me give you an example.

A company we have been working with, called Collinson, has a division that enhances airline and travel experiences. When the airports shut down during the Covid pandemic, they quickly realised that their lounges weren't going to generate any income for quite a period of time. This has been disastrous for most businesses working in the travel industry.

In the misery of a board meeting, someone made a throwaway comment about how the company would be better off turning all the airport lounges into testing areas, where incoming passengers could take Covid-19 tests and get the results quickly, in order to check if they were safe to enter the country. This promised a functional purpose for their airport lounges, and potential income as well. As Plato almost said: necessity is the mother of invention!

DISNEY'S SPLIT PERSONALITY

There have been many historical examples of the close relationship between arts and business and of how skills in one domain can easily filter into the other. If we go back to the 1950s, Walt Disney coined the expression 'imagineering', which defined the link between creating something and ultimately realising it. Indeed, when we think of Disney, we have the perfect example of someone who morphed between an artist and a creative entrepreneur. People who were familiar with him claimed that he had three different personas, which were quite separate from each other. There was Walt the dreamer, Walt the realist, and Walt the critic – and you never knew which one was coming to a meeting!

Disney went to great lengths to cultivate these differing sides of his nature. He designed different rooms, which he worked in separately with his teams, in order to encourage these various behaviours. He was disciplined enough that he wouldn't allow any thoughts from one of the 'other Walts' to creep into his mindset when he was working on a different sector. To punctuate it with more certainty, he would bring in team members who would amplify the debate at each stage; he would only allow people to brainstorm and voice ideas without criticism in his creative room, leaving him to get practical in his realist room and become a fearsome cynic in his critic room. That way, he could be assured of true clarity of thought at all stages of his projects.

This is a fascinating insight into the way that the creative and entrepreneurial mindset can merge in one individual, and how this obsession with a singular focus, combined with his tenacity, are perhaps significant reasons for the monumental success that Walt Disney managed to achieve.

ENCOURAGING CREATIVITY

Having established that creativity is a valuable entity for any business or commercial enterprise, it's clear that encouraging this creative process doesn't come naturally to many business-people and that changing that mindset is a big challenge. So what's the best way to encourage creativity in an organisation where everybody is different?

Firstly, you should ensure there is a safety net in place for when people make mistakes, so that bad things don't happen to them if they try out new ideas. Both truly creative geniuses and brilliant businesspeople are known for their risk-taking natures and, when you're willing to try out new plans, you have to accept that they won't always work out. That's absolutely fine. However, while we all want to steer towards successful ideas as quickly as possible, it's also important that you shouldn't stifle the creative process by punishing a few early mistakes. There must be room for these people to breathe, otherwise their creative juices will never flow. If they are criticised or punished for getting things wrong, they'll soon stop trying.

To help this process, try to find a way of protecting your core business while you are tinkering with new things for the first time and, as you go through this process, simply hold on to the ideas that work best. You need to adopt a healthy attitude that failure is just a way of discovering that something didn't work; be ready to move on from that experience, accepting that it is merely part of the overall creative process.

I think it is also reasonable to assert that creative people can sometimes be a little sensitive, so you need to nurture their talents with excellent people management. You will soon dampen down the creative spirit if you establish an environment in which people are laughed at or belittled if they suggest something obscure or seemingly bizarre, which doesn't obviously lead to a eureka moment.

There are plenty of examples of businesses encouraging creativity, but the Heinz corporation perhaps provides us with the most dramatic example. Some years ago, I was lucky enough to be invited to an Inc 500 conference in Pittsburgh. The conference was a celebration for the 500 fastest growing companies in America, and at the time I was working with one of the companies that had made the list. A speaker explained that at one time during the early history of Heinz, the company had developed a culture where they fired a cannon into the air when someone messed up badly, celebrating the error. The people of Pittsburgh could hear the blast and felt relief that another mistake had been made and they were relieved to know that their jobs would be safe for a while longer. I'm not a great believer in weapons in the workplace, but it's the most extreme example I've heard to remind us that we should celebrate creativity and not punish people for taking risks that don't work out.

Cultures form by accident – not just as a result of the rules companies make, but also by people noticing the emphasis that is put on everyday occurrences. Don't let that happen. Eat the pudding first! Decide what culture you want, create it yourself and work backwards, paying attention to the weak signals. Most companies have stories that are passed from worker to worker about something extraordinary that happened with a customer or an unusual incident that makes people smile. Encourage those stories; they often reinforce the personality of the business for all members of staff at all levels of the business. This is your opportunity to get creative! It's possible to set up all manner of staff schemes in order to reward new ideas and this will be truly appreciated by your employees, not merely encouraging them to be creative but also improving buy-in and general morale.

EXITING YOUR COMFORT ZONE

You also need to be willing to take yourself out of your comfort zone and encourage others to do the same. The reality is that creativity often emanates from a place of uncertainty and worry, and it's difficult to insulate yourself against this negative sensation. You have to be willing to push yourself, you have to be willing to think outside of the box and you have to tolerate some of the pain and suffering that can be associated with these processes feeling unnatural.

Another great option that I would recommend for businesses is to hire a board member from the arts community, so you can spice up the creativity of your meetings. This can be a reciprocal relationship, with you offering to do the same for them. Arts companies almost always welcome input from the business community and can often garner commercial benefits from the two-way discourse.

Finally, you should nurture your own brain by trying something new. Many adults are wary of taking on an entirely new skill in later life, but there's nothing more liberating than becoming proficient in something you've never done previously. Nothing gets the creative juices flowing faster! Learn another language, take up a musical instrument, dance, cook, play chess, learn to fly a plane… anything that gets you out of your comfort zone and routine behaviour.

Not only will the things I've suggested here help your business to be more successful, but the process will be fun and worthwhile. The sense of accomplishment that you will generate will be life enriching and you will grow as a human being, becoming more open to new experiences and ideas. That is surely a benefit that goes well beyond profitability and commercial success.

CONCLUSIONS

By now you should have realised that you do have the capability to start your own business if you want to, and that you don't need to come up with an earth-shattering new idea to be successful. Perhaps you've given some thought to the actual business you'll set up and what it will specialise in. You may already have an idea about the people you'll need in your camp to help you. I hope you've dared to dream about where the decision to aim high and start something from scratch may lead, and the benefits it will bring to you and your family when you achieve financial security for life. You've started to begin with the end in mind and to eat the pudding first. You need to condense all of this into a plan that you can follow and execute without distraction.

I've created a resource that will help you do exactly that. A series of strategic business questions that distils the core components that will give you a bespoke plan to shape your idea into a business that you can scale and sell. You can get it at:

www.garyashworth.com/eatthepuddingfirst

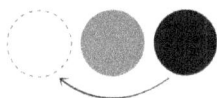

SCALE

"GROWTH IS NEVER BY MERE CHANCE;
IT IS THE RESULT OF FORCES WORKING
TOGETHER."

James Cash Penney – founder, JC Penney

I enjoyed writing this section the most, since scaling can make the greatest difference and the chapters here are the most valuable.

Getting this phase of growth right can lead to an 'all you can dream of' outcome with the right team assembled, a clear plan, marketing that outpaces your competitors and the assertive execution of urgent goals. It should be fun, too. It will define you!

However, remember that 'What got us here won't get us there.'

Scaling a business requires a different mindset than starting one, and that often leads to a different team of managers, salespeople and executives and a more complex level of financial control.

Most of the lessons within this section are taken from my own experience, relating to when I floated a business on the London Stock Market and decided to 'go for it', right up to the time I sold it to a trade buyer for 10 times the float price four years later.

If we were to hit our goals, we needed to hire more than 200 staff in a two-year period and work out how we could raise the cash to acquire businesses for lower multiples of profits than our own stock market rating. It meant hiring trainers and running an academy for graduates and, through trial and error, working out the core competencies they possessed that would give them a chance of success. I say 'we' because I couldn't have done it by myself. The business needed new skills that I didn't have. I hired a non-executive director, who introduced me to City advisors and taught me the idiosyncrasies of debt financing, arrangement fees and interest coupons. It was all double Dutch to me at first, but I was forced to learn fast or appear naïve and be taken advantage of. I gave 5% equity to this guy, because I knew he had the experience and knowledge to help me, and I wanted him to have a financial interest that would be aligned with my own. I wanted him to worry about the same things that kept me up at night. It was the right decision; we became the fastest growing company on the junior market, two years in a row.

The rest of the lessons – perhaps the most valuable of all – are taken from what I've learned when I've got things wrong; I vowed never to make the same mistakes again.

I've acquired businesses without doing thorough enough diligence. I've been defrauded, backed the wrong people and invested in sectors where I didn't have enough experience to make the correct judgement. These were the hardest lessons to learn, and the ones from which I still carry the battle scars. I describe them in detail so that you can avoid them.

For example: some of your staff will grow with the business and develop their skills, but some won't be able to keep up, and now is not the time to be sentimental. It's not just a case of loyalty. There can be amicable solutions if you've outgrown some of the people who helped you in the beginning. They won't be comfortable anyway if they're out of their depth, and you won't want to stop the train as it speeds along the track.

It's amazing that so many people get stuck here; some get bogged down for years. I have been guilty of getting locked into this zone – it's warm and familiar and friendly – but it's also quite challenging because you've not jumped that next hurdle yet.

Don't make the same mistake.

It's at this point that hiring a non-executive director can help remind you of your goals. These should be written down by now, with clear timeframes attached. They may be different goals from the ones you started with; you've reached base camp, but now it's time to attack the summit!

They can remind you to 'Eat the pudding first!'

We learn about the importance of pace and the tragedy of procrastination. We also discuss your relationship with the bank and try to understand the way banks think.

Growing a successful business gives you options. It's hard work, but when it's done, it allows you to make choices that suit your lifestyle. It defines you. It teaches you new levels of tenacity you didn't think yourself capable of.

- You may be building a business to sell it and achieve financial security for life for you and anyone else you care to share it with.

- You may choose to reinvest the profits into an ambitious growth strategy.

- Alternatively, once your company reaches a certain level of profitability, you may choose to cruise along and do just enough to enjoy the lifestyle, feeding the profits you have earned into your personal piggy bank.

- You may want to install a competent management team who will keep an eye on things while you do something completely different.

- You may want to build a dynasty – something you can bring your children into, to look after the next generation.

There's no right or wrong answer – that's what is so great about running your own business. Instead of being someone else's employee and marching to the beat of their drum, you get to decide your own fate. You don't need to keep buying lottery tickets, studying tea leaves or gazing into a crystal ball.

I've learned to reduce the chance of failure along the way, and I want to share techniques that will ensure you don't need to risk everything to grow quickly. You can test markets first, and only invest heavily when the odds are in your favour.

"TRY LOTS OF DIFFERENT THINGS AND KEEP WHAT WORKS."

It's in this section of the book that you will learn to harness your time with the business outcomes you seek. We'll explore how you can plan the best way of getting work done through other people – and, most importantly, we will discuss what happens when you get to that target; once you have made it, you don't want to blow it. After all, investing your profits badly can put you all the way back to Day 1.

In reality, the challenges are very different in this phase of growth compared with the straightforward nature of the things we focused on in start-up mode. Unless we break them down into bite-sized chunks, there is a real chance that we might be overwhelmed by the complexity of the journey.

We start to realise that:

"THERE'S SELDOM AN UNACHIEVABLE GOAL; JUST AN UNACHIEVABLE TIMEFRAME."

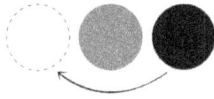

EMBRACING FAILURE

"A PERSON WHO NEVER MADE A MISTAKE
NEVER TRIED ANYTHING NEW."

Albert Einstein

Half of business start-ups fail within the first five years, if you believe all that is written in the *Daily Telegraph*. If you're going to enter into this world, you have to accept that there are risks, but with careful planning you can reduce them substantially. Everything that is worth doing in life has a risk. It's how we learn. Kids fall out of trees and adults fall off bicycles and occasionally have road accidents. Walkers get struck by lightning; houses catch fire. It's not a reason to stay in bed worrying all day; you must accept that failing is okay. A person who never failed at anything never tried anything at all.

Let's drill down and examine that statistic: 50% of business start-ups fail within five years. Firstly, among this figure are a whole bunch of people who have absolutely no idea what they're doing. They're trying to drive the car without ever taking a single lesson. Most of these businesses are among the 20% that fail in the very first year of their existence. Even by reading a book about the subject, you've shown that you understand there's help available.

Advantage you!

By reading this particular book and downloading the template available at the end, you have a significant advantage. I genuinely believe that absorbing the information contained in these pages will reduce the odds of your business failing to below 20%. Or, if you wish to express this in more positive terms, your chance of success will now exceed 80%. Better odds than you're ever likely to encounter in a casino.

When you consider setting up a business for the first time, there is inevitably a huge amount of emotion flying around. There is a fear of failure, and an equal fear of the unknown. It goes against the grain of everything you've done so far in your life, and probably everything most of your family and peers are doing, too. You may not receive helpful or encouraging advice from those who don't know or haven't done it. You might be told that you're making a massive mistake. People are frightened of the unknown – which is good, because it leaves more space for people like us who are prepared to take the plunge.

All these factors tend to provoke an emotional state in the budding entrepreneur. Let's put that baggage down right now and leave it all behind; instead of approaching this from an emotional perspective, let's examine it rationally.

In business we can choose to stop doing the things that don't work and focus more on the things that do. In fact, when we have proved they work, we can bet heavily on them. Simply by implementing this straightforward strategy, you've moved the odds of success decisively in your favour. You've set yourself on the path for both your business and your life to be far more successful. It's not rocket science, but it *is* science. It's actually quite straightforward.

WHAT IF I HAD NEVER TRIED IT?

In order to do this, we need to radically alter our relationship with failure. Rather than fearing failure, we must learn to love and embrace it and recognise that it is a critical step on the path to success. Only by experiencing our fair share of failure can we learn what does and doesn't work. We need to be grateful for each and every one of these lessons, because they make us better. Cultivating a positive mindset is key. You can't win the lottery unless you buy a ticket! You've got to be in it to win it.

I would argue that one of the most depressing qualities a person can have, not just in business but generally in life, is a reluctance to try something due to the fear of failure. This is a paralysing characteristic that hamstrings many potentially exciting business ideas before they even get off the ground. So many potential entrepreneurs deny themselves the opportunity to find out what would have happened if they had only tried. I am reminded of the title of the autobiography of world champion motorcyclist Valentino Rossi: *What If I Had Never Tried It?*

This doesn't only apply to Italian motorcycling geniuses; it applies in every walk of life. If you don't try something, you'll never know what you are capable of achieving. You could discover something that turns your life from ordinary into extraordinary.

The interesting thing is that this cautious mentality that grips so many people is the exact opposite of our mindset in our early years. We're encouraged to experiment from an early age, while growing up at home and then again at school. In fact, if we don't experiment sufficiently, we will never develop the basic life skills that are essential for our survival. Our growing brains require constant input in order to reach anything approaching their full potential, and children possess an unending thirst for knowledge and stimulation.

The ongoing quest

This helps us in our ongoing quest to find out what works for us and what skills we have a natural affinity for. We try a range of different sports and see which ones mesh with our inbuilt abilities. For example, the infamous and hugely successful American track athlete Mary Decker started running simply because, by her own admission, she was useless at all ball games. At some point, most of us will have the chance to participate in drama groups, public speaking, or singing to see how we get on in front of an audience. It's the same with musical instruments and we should, of course, grasp the opportunities that suit us. Who knows when we'll hit upon a particular talent?

This tendency can also be seen in academia. From a young age, we pick a variety of subjects in school, with more choice available now than ever before, but we will naturally gravitate towards certain topics or skills at which we excel. This will become the backbone of our personality, and the things we choose will define the rich tapestry of our makeup. They could then lead to a career of our choosing. It may very well be that we fail in many areas outside of a few core skills. That doesn't matter in the slightest. Failure is never seen as a bad thing in any of these contexts; it is instead viewed as an essential part of our learning and decision-making process, as any parent will know who has listened, hands over their ears, to their child's violin scratching its way through *Twinkle, Twinkle Little Star*.

If we don't try things, we will never know whether we can succeed at them. This is a theme that dominates our young lives. As we get older, we can get set in our ways. We ask fewer questions. We find familiarity in our routines and don't experiment as often. If we're wise and crave a richer life, we should keep experimenting, from cradle to grave. Let's have more fun while we're on this planet. We're all a long time dead!

PROBLEM TERM

Re-examining the concept of failure, I admit that I have a problem with this particular word. It's so negative. The word 'failure' has such miserable connotations that I believe it leads to people giving up much more quickly than they otherwise would. If things don't work out first time, many people assume they have failed and never try again. This isn't a great philosophy at all, since no one has ever become outstanding at any pursuit in a matter of days. It takes years and years of practice in order to excel at anything remotely worthwhile.

Let's frame the word 'failure' differently. Let's associate it with experimentation and link it to that idea instead. We would then view the circumstances in a different light and be encouraged to persevere further. Everyone knows that you have to experiment for a while before you hit upon the right formula. This is why bands make tuneless rackets in garages until they eventually hit upon a sound that carries them to musical success and stardom. It's why Thomas Edison made 1,000 unsuccessful attempts at inventing the lightbulb before he discovered that it needed a vacuum to stop the filament from burning out.

On a more mundane level, if you talk to people who have stopped smoking, they will happily tell you that they failed many times before they finally managed to quit the habit for good. The average smoker fails to quit six or seven times on average before they finally succeed. That should still be considered cause for celebration, not criticism just because these people didn't succeed the very first time. Every time we fail, we find 'another way not to do something' and we make a further step towards our ultimate goal. Instead of beating ourselves up, we should be proud of our tenacity and industrious nature.

Failure and rejection

Another problem with the word 'failure' is that it is intrinsically linked with rejection – a painful human condition that we certainly don't enjoy. Our brains are hardwired to avoid rejection wherever possible, which is why it damages our soul so profoundly. We tend to confuse business failure with personal failure, though, when the two aren't remotely similar.

If you give your heart to someone you love and they reject you, it hurts and it can be earth-shattering. Those arrows pierce the skin and leave scars. By comparison, if we leave a message and no one calls us back, or we present to a client and they go with a different proposition, or we introduce a new sales line or service that doesn't work, it's no big deal. We'll just try something else. Those arrows should bounce off the skin so easily that we barely notice them.

The truth is that failing is good. Try different things on a regular basis. Be willing to experiment with ideas that don't disturb the core business or put jobs and profits at risk. This will allow you to become accustomed to the process of experimentation and will ensure that you are constantly improving your product or service offering.

This is the opposite of a poker player going all in. If you stick all your chips in the middle of the table, you either need to be pretty certain that you're going to win, or there's a chance you might lose everything. This doesn't apply in business. In this much more sophisticated world, you can make thousands of inconsequential small bets, so you can test the market, before you finally take the plunge and the big risks, safe in the knowledge that you're doing so from an informed perspective. You're effectively only betting when the odds are substantially in your favour.

NURTURING BRILLIANCE

Brilliance and brilliant ideas seldom just appear out of nowhere. If you do find an excellent idea, something that works swimmingly, it's unlikely to function perfectly straight out of the gate. Even the best racehorse requires some time to reach its full gallop. Ideas and plans are inevitably improved by reworking, refining and tweaking. This means that failure, as we choose to describe it, is an integral part of the most successful concepts. Ideas may vaguely work immediately, but failure often makes them great.

In his book *Outliers*, the author and journalist Malcolm Gladwell examines people with exceptional skills and argues that they still need to invest 10,000 hours of practice in order to reach a world-class level. Every raw talent needs failure and practice in order to become the best. Chess players aren't grand masters as soon as they take the pieces out of the box for the first time.

The Beatles didn't suddenly write hit albums and some of the most memorable songs in music history overnight. They learned their instruments, diligently practised writing songs, and invested well over 10,000 hours in their craft. They even spent two years performing covers and some of their own early material for several hours every day at a variety of seedy clubs in Germany. The Beatles were not an overnight success. Beatlemania was not instant.

These are just some examples of people who have triumphed after initially struggling to reach the apex of their ambition, and in many cases failing dramatically. Here are some other famous names who endured challenges before they made it to the top:

- **Bill Gates**: Dropped out of Harvard and started a failed first business called Traf-O-Data with Microsoft co-founder Paul Allen.

- **Henry Ford:** Failed in his early businesses, which left him broke five times, before he founded the successful Ford Motor Company.

- **Walt Disney:** Was fired by a newspaper because 'he lacked imagination and had no good ideas.'

- **Fred Astaire:** In his first screen test, the testing director of MGM described one of the greatest screen icons of all time like this: 'Can't act. Can't sing. Slightly bald. Can dance a little.'

- **Vincent Van Gogh:** Possibly the most revered artist ever – but sold only one painting during his lifetime.

- **Elvis Presley:** In 1954, Elvis was still a nobody. Jimmy Denny, manager of the Grand Ole Opry, fired him after just one performance, telling him: 'You ain't going nowhere, son. You ought to go back to driving a truck.'

These are just a handful of examples. There are thousands of others I could have mentioned. What's the worst that can happen?

I keep reiterating the same mantra: it's always wise to try lots of different things and keep those that work. Sometimes it helps to ask, 'What's the worst that can happen if things don't work out?' You'll usually find that the earth will continue revolving no matter how great your so-called failures may be; and, if the core of the business isn't affected by mistakes, it's easy to keep trying new things until you find something that makes a difference. Most successful people do this without realising they're doing it. It's the business version of nature's 'survival of the fittest'.

This means that it is crucially important to build a culture in your workplace that embraces experimentation and failure. If people are slammed, criticised or even fired when things go wrong, inevitably your workforce will rapidly stop coming up with new ideas. This will have a virtual Pavlovian impact on your business and will scupper its potential, since great ideas from employees won't ever be heard.

In his new book, *Work Rules!*, Google's Head of People Operations, Laszlo Bock, states that 'It's also important to reward failure' in order to encourage risk-taking. Making mistakes isn't something that should be chastised; it's something that should be positively encouraged. Small failures do not need to represent a crisis. They can be learning experiences that will nourish your business for years to come.

Learn to fail fast, though. Don't keep making the same mistakes again and again while hoping for a different outcome.

The key judgement is to try things thoroughly enough to give them a chance of working, but shut them down (whatever the emotional or financial investment) once it's become apparent that they won't.

If you really are riding a dead horse, get off.

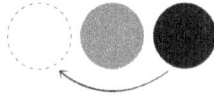

CONTROLS AND MEASURES

**"YOU CAN'T MANAGE
WHAT YOU CAN'T MEASURE."**

Peter Drucker

What gets measured gets done.

What gets paid for gets done more.

What gets paid a hell of a lot for gets done a hell of a lot more.

I can state with 100% confidence that this applies across all industries!

This means that controlling and measuring aspects of businesses is imperative for their success. However, it's more important to ensure that we measure the right things and don't take too many factors into consideration. When you're going through the process of deciding which items need measuring, the list must be ruthlessly edited in order to ensure you focus on the key aspects that really make a difference. These must be in alignment with corporate goals if the process is to be successful and relevant. Keep it simple – if you can.

Having company-wide measurements effectively hands over the rule book from you as the business owner to the company itself, so that things trundle along effectively without your input. This then empowers your staff to take their own decisions and get work done without checking with you first.

What you will have then is a more autonomous and self-managing organisation. Employees will keep the business consistent and accountable, tracking costs and sales while measuring efficiency and producing accounting data. They will also ensure that this information is kept safe. It is all critical information, so it's important that you put these processes in place meticulously and that you manage your staff assiduously to hit the timetables set. Late data should be a warning sign of bad news.

You will not be able to scale up your business effectively if these controls are not put in place correctly. I cannot over-emphasise the importance of delivering this aspect of your operation with

"

IT'S EASY TO GET BOGGED DOWN

IN DATA AND OVER-ANALYSE.

KEEP IT SIMPLE AND EFFECTIVE.

"

diligence and accuracy. The data needs to make sense to your workforce and must be produced as regularly as clockwork. Your staff are the ones who will be collating the data and, if they know you won't be impressed with the results, it might help them to change their behaviour to meet goals rather than be criticised for not hitting targets set.

Controls and measures play a fundamental role in our everyday lives. This starts at school; we begin to measure our proficiency from a very early age, where testing and grading is an inbuilt part of the process. As we grow older, credit ratings, insurance premiums and life assurance rates are all calculated using data held and analysed. There's been an explosion in data capture, where lakes of data are stored, analysed, sliced and diced to try to predict trends and our future habits before we even know ourselves. It's a sinister practice, but one that's here to stay.

Whether you're playing chess online, booking theatre tickets, complaining about your local councillor, or selling goods on Amazon, your data all gets measured, traded and sold on.

ADVANTAGES OF CONTROLS AND MEASURES

The advantages of controlling and tracking our data are clear. Measuring provides us with a real insight into the quantitative and qualitative values of certain datasets. It effectively tells us whether something is good, mediocre, poor or great! This then can be used externally as a measure of value, or as a way for the individual to improve their performance. Controls naturally radiate outwards from this measurement, as we develop systems to take advantage of this kind of valuable information.

It's easy to get bogged down in data and over-analyse. Keep it simple and effective.

In business, the key is to define only the key levers that you use to measure and drive the business. Edit them ruthlessly to as few as possible. Just think about what you need to see and how often you need to see it.

Individuals and managers might simply need to measure sales activity, bids, customers won and lost and margins on a daily basis. The board may want to measure costs, stock, cash, profits, trends and competitor analysis monthly. Marketing will have their own measurement set; so will IT, HR, legal and every other part of your business. As an owner, whether you're in the start-up or scale phase of growing your business, what's important is to be able to deep dive into the data when things veer off plan, understanding the reasons why the problem occurred and fixing it quickly. When we win, why do we win? When we lose, why did we lose?

Few enterprises in any area of life succeed without a clear notion of where they're headed and what they hope to achieve. You don't just start walking – you have a clear goal of where you're going. People don't just start painting their houses – they have a clear vision of how the room will look when they're finished.

I remember as a child watching *Blue Peter* on television and seeing the progress each week as a totaliser board lit up to show how their charity campaigns were getting closer and closer to their end goal. Only *Blue Peter* could turn 225 tons of scrap metal into two centres for the elderly and eight hot dinner vans!

The same applies to business. As you set off on your entrepreneurial journey, you will almost inevitably have certain things you want to achieve. You might want to experience total financial freedom. You might wish to purchase a key asset, like a bigger house. You might desire a particular lifestyle. You might be aiming for a certain level of cash in the bank. Regardless of your aim, controls and measures provide insightful indicators of where you are on your journey to success.

TYPES OF CONTROLS AND MEASURES

As a general rule, measures tend to fall into the following three categories: dashboards, procedures and automated systems.

Dashboards

These are visual scorecards that provide what is effectively real-time data for key performance indicators. The particular KPIs can vary quite significantly from one business to another, but they may include such factors as:

* Revenue and margin totals

- Sales calls

- Volume of customers

- Project variance schedules

- Customer lifetime values.

A dashboard is your 'at a glance snapshot' to see how well your business is doing, and it provides an extremely valuable window into the level of performance you are achieving. When this form of measurement is implemented successfully, it should act as an early warning system, enabling you to notice problems quickly so that you can take swift action to remedy them.

Procedures

These are process controls that define known pathways of daily behaviours. This is the time where expectations are set, defining standards for both management and staff.

They set out rules for everyone, making sure laws and regulations are adhered to and spelling out regulations for health and safety, environment policies, sickness and holidays, and so on. They will also let employees know where they can turn to for help.

Procedures are often defined in a corporate employee handbook. They should also protect the company from employee claims. These rules play an important legal aspect of any successful business.

Automated systems

These are embedded controls that can't be altered or overwritten. They generally give clarification of the work routines that need to be performed, and define efficient processes that have been worked out as best practice.

Any process automation in the business should serve the purpose of saving time and reducing mistakes – but it should also be forcing the segregation of tasks, in order to reduce opportunities for fraud within the company.

These fixed processes should also ensure consistency of results, empowering the people following the tasks and liberating them to work elsewhere in the business. Automation serves the purpose of freeing up your talent to participate in defined and creative work.

THE VALUE OF CONTROLS AND MEASURES

This is one business lesson that I learned the hard way. Along with a business partner, I once bought one of London's most popular nightspots, the Atlantic Bar and Grill. This was a restaurant and nightclub with a 3am license and a huge capacity. It was a fire sale from the administrator, but we felt we could restore the brand to its former glory.

However, despite our optimism, it wasn't a sector I knew particularly well and I made a disastrous mistake right at the beginning: I hired an accountant without taking references. They were convincing at the interview stage, so we went ahead. Initially, management accounts, profits and cash balances seemed above board, but we subsequently found out that he was less than honest. He was a crook.

The appropriate controls, dashboard and measurements weren't put in place, so it all ended rather disastrously. Although we didn't lose money during the time that we owned the business, we didn't make any either. I've really no idea where the cash and profit disappeared to. I'm ashamed to say that it was my own fault for not having the correct daily, weekly and monthly measures in place.

Frighteningly, some years later I read that the same accountant had been arrested as part of a huge £200 million corporate fraud investigation. His face was plastered all over the newspapers, so his immediate future in accountancy appeared to be rather limited. Fraudsters can be clever people, who cover their tracks well and are often not rumbled for years. Please double check when trusting financial leaders. I hope, by my making this serious mistake, that you won't do the same. Be paranoid about financial control.

The appropriate auditing and segregation of duties and the ruthless implementation of controls could have ensured a different result for me. I learned the hard way, and I won't make the same mistake again – although they are famous last words!

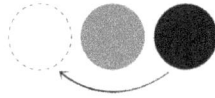

BRANDING, MARKETING, WEBSITE, SOCIAL MEDIA AND CONTENT

"GOOD MARKETING MAKES YOU LOOK SMART. GREAT MARKETING MAKES THE CUSTOMER FEEL SMART."

Joe Chernov

In this digital age, marketing has arguably never been more important. Standing out from the crowd has become a massive challenge in what is an increasingly globalised business environment. Competing in this climate has necessitated seeking a blend of in-house production and hired external help. As an

"

MARKETING CAN BE

VIEWED AS THE LAS VEGAS

OF BUSINESS!

"

entrepreneur, the responsibility lies on your shoulders to weigh up the costs and benefits of your approach before deciding on the appropriate blend for your particular business.

BRAND AUDIT

Stop right there! Before you invest any money in colour brochures or marketing plans, it's always sensible to conduct an audit in order to define your own brand. Design has become such a critical part of the business landscape in recent years, so this needs some consideration before any decisions are made. You need to think about your target audience: who are you attempting to attract, and what marketing message might convey this in the best way possible?

There are several ways to approach the process of deciding this, but the best place to start is to consult your existing customers. Identify a way of surveying people who are already working with you and you will quickly gain an impression of the people you'd like to deal with in the future. It's also important to think about insightful questions that you could level at your existing people. What do your competitors think of you? How do your own staff perceive your brand? Is there anything you could be doing better? Treat the activity of connecting with your customers as an ongoing process and you will constantly identify new and exciting ways of communicating your message to potential clients.

On the other hand, some companies have already done an excellent job of defining their personality in the marketplace. If you find yourself in this position and already intimately understand what your brand represents, you should definitely tread carefully before changing or adding to your existing messaging. Marketing is one area where you can burn through a vast amount of cash in a short period of time, all while doing things that are actually detrimental to your wellbeing. Marketing can be viewed as the Las Vegas of business! Make sure you know what is working and what is not working before you embark on this process.

If you're going to hire outside assistance for your marketing campaigns, here is a word of warning: marketing people often talk a load of twaddle! They will cite marketing or website statistics that are difficult or impossible to disprove, although they may ultimately have minimal impact on your actual business.

Identifying a statistical basis for marketing can be an extremely prickly subject and so I would rather rely on an insight that I've gleaned over the years. In my experience, good marketing people are usually slightly mad! They are certainly creative and definitely look at things from a left-field perspective. Paying heed to this observation will give you an excellent template for identifying someone who can assist your business.

It's also definitely advisable to tweak your branding on a relatively regular basis. Even the most successful companies in the world – hugely established names like Amazon, Google and Coca-Cola – refine and update their image over time.

WHAT'S THE COMPETITION DOING?

As important as your own message is to your success, you must also acknowledge that your brand doesn't exist in a vacuum. You can only be successful in business relative to others, and your brand will be continually compared with the competition. How will you stand out from the crowd? How will you go further than all the others? What have you established that is distinctive and unique?

This means that the first impression the customer has of your company must be immediately memorable. It must also significantly differentiate you from other competitors in the marketplace. This can begin with the most basic aspects – it could be as simple as an attractive logo or appealing colour palette – but you can also set yourself apart by producing interesting content that customers identify with, or even a catchphrase that sticks around for generations.

An excellent example of this concerns the well-known car rental company Avis. The firm was looking to differentiate itself from its rivals in a fiercely competitive market, but it faced something of a logistical problem. Their cars weren't better, their locations were broadly the same, and their pricing wasn't especially competitive. They were always in second place behind Hertz. Their ad agency, Doyle Dane Bernbach, came up with the tagline 'When you're only No. 2, you try harder.' The 'We Try Harder' ads were an instant hit. Within a year, Avis went from losing $3.2m to earning $1.2m – the first time it had been profitable in more than a decade. It was so successful that they kept the slogan for 50 years, illustrating just how successful an advertising and marketing campaign can be if you get the tone spot on.

MAKE YOUR SERVICE OR PRODUCT EASY TO BUY

Visibility is an incredibly important aspect of any business. No one can purchase your product if they can't find it. This means that strong website search engine optimisation (SEO) and Google AdWords implementation are absolutely essential. You must ensure that the name of your business comes up regularly when customers search for keywords and key issues in your particular industry. It has to be easy for customers to find you, and when they do, your website must be easy to navigate. It can take some specialised experience for you to achieve this, so hiring someone with a proven track record is the thing to do.

On top of this, the way your site is set up is also vitally important. The purchase procedure needs to be transparent and the return policy straightforward. Remember, as well, that the web-browsing public have little patience. They will soon give up and go elsewhere if your site is too cluttered. Remember the *three-click rule*, which is an unofficial rule concerning the design of website navigation. It recommends that a visitor to a website should be able to find any information they need with no more than three mouse clicks, based on the belief that users of a site will become frustrated and often leave if they cannot find the information within that time. Make sure that your website is user friendly.

Seek feedback, constantly refine your site and stay ahead of the competition.

TAKE IT TO THE PEOPLE

Once you're happy with the look and feel of your brand and your website is complete, it's time to tell the world about your business using adverts, slogans and social media presence. This process all starts at home, though. Do your stationery, business cards, presentations and proposals adequately reflect your new style? Does your office or sales outlet show the same consistency? Your staff are a reflection of your brand, too; have you trained them to embody the same values that your brand represents?

Branding is all about creating a uniform impression across all facets of a business, so it really does require attention to detail in order to ensure that your tone and messaging are correct at all times. If you can make the process fun and enjoyable for employees as well, they're much more likely to buy in to the whole rebranding, rather than being cynical and obstructive.

Social media and data

Content has become an almost ubiquitous buzzword online – and with good reason. Companies and brands across every conceivable niche are producing their own content on a regular basis, before distributing it widely, and there is a huge market for this content.

This process achieves two primary goals. Firstly, producing quality content demonstrates that you are an expert in your field and a trustworthy source of knowledge in everything that you do. Secondly, it's a constant reminder to both existing and potential customers that you are active and doing regular business.

Most companies now utilise social media platforms and other content-sharing avenues. For example, one recruitment business that I'm involved with aims to put out three messages per day via LinkedIn. It's their way of keeping connected to customers and it's an effective way of differentiating the company from competitors, while showing its audience that the business remains at the cutting edge of the industry.

LinkedIn, Twitter, Snapchat, Instagram, Facebook and, more recently, Clubhouse are all excellent platforms to distribute content and connect with an audience. It's important to note that the approach to social media content is fundamentally different from the approach to traditional media. You don't want to post things that have been carefully cultivated by an advertising agency. In this modern digital world, where everything can be faked or photoshopped, authenticity is an extremely valuable commodity. DIY posts are sometimes preferred.

Equally, don't just post from a business perspective. Providing some personal content shows that you are human and reveals a more intimate side of your business. One thing that is certain is that people continue to buy from brands, companies and organisations they trust and like. Cultivating this sort of connection with them is particularly valuable, yet it can be achieved with a small amount of effort.

Blogs, podcasts, surveys, straw polls, event sponsorship, thought leadership pieces, community work – they all keep you in the limelight. Any content is a constant reminder to your audience that you're still out there and current.

Your thoughts and the success of your attempts to connect with your community are also important. You should be setting yourself targets for social media and then making sure you meet them, in a similar way to how you would with sales targets. Monitoring this all takes time, and allowances need to be made when taking time out of people's busy days.

We've talked in previous chapters about the collection and interpretation of data and how it's become an imperative part of understanding customer behaviour and habits, whether this is in the analysis of the people looking at your website or the people calling you. This isn't something that you can jettison or ignore. Building up lists of existing, potential and past customers is another important part of the process, which will help you to reach a deeper audience of people.

Searching questions

If you're not brave enough to ask your customers these two simple (but key) questions regularly, then you should fire yourself and change your job:

- How are we doing?

- What could we do better?

I'm constantly surprised how many businesses seem to be in denial or argue back when you give them genuine feedback about poor service or ideas for improvement. As a customer, it's easier to say nothing, walk away and never deal with that company again.

A better mindset would be 'There's never any criticism, only feedback.'

Feedback is a gift; it tells you how to improve your business. It's free advice from someone who has experienced your service. It's a clue to help you make a better business.

You should be constantly evaluating every aspect of your operation and, of course, attempting to improve your business on a continual basis. There are many ways to ask these questions, but they unquestionably hold the key to what you need to do to improve your business. Don't ask your colleagues. Don't ask the board. In fact, don't ask anyone other than your customers. The feedback you receive from customers is invaluable data, and it's something you should be continually collating, collecting and thinking about.

Here's an extreme example of using feedback to grow profits. Some years ago, I attended a conference hosted by the publishing company Marshall Cavendish, who were experts in direct marketing and list brokers. It was alarming in the way it demonstrated the power of direct marketing (of course, all of this took place before the recent regulations were introduced regarding the storage and utilisation of personal data). Marshall Cavendish had a request to see how much it would cost to rent out their complaints and opt-out list. Effectively, they were proposing to pay in order to get in contact with the sort of stroppy and angry people who had specifically taken the time to write and complain about being contacted. These were people who had expressed the sentiment that they never wanted to be contacted again, in any circumstances, about anything at all.

It seemed like madness, but the company in question knew its audience, and a deal was done. The list was procured by a company that sold handguns via direct mail, and the campaign was magnificently successful. These complainers ideally fitted the profile of potential gun buyers and fitted into the demographic of potential customers perfectly. It's a sinister fact of life that there are lists for everything and anyone.

DISASTER TIME

Marketing isn't easy. I've had my own fair share of marketing disasters. Before you dip your toes into the pool of persuasion, it's important to carefully consider the consequences of your campaigns.

One example that still haunts me is the time I sent an aspirin attached to a mailshot to 10,000 people on my mailing list. The gist of this was that aspirin tablets help people get rid of short-term headaches, but that working with my company got rid of long-term headaches. Cute, right?

Not exactly. There were two results from this campaign and neither of them were particularly helpful. First, the post office put the letters through a franking machine, which crushed all of the tablets to powder. That was bad enough... but second, during the very same week, letters containing the deadly chemical powder anthrax were sent to random people in the post. Five people were killed, and the story became a major media talking point.

On the morning that our potential and existing clients opened the letters and spilled powder over themselves, there was mild hysteria and the phones started ringing. All we achieved by sending out aspirin tablets was to terrify many potential and existing customers – and the consequences didn't stop there. Happy shiny customers stopped dealing with us and told their friends how irresponsible we were, complaining that our intentions were irresponsible and dangerous. We were lucky not to be denounced as a terrorist organisation and added to the US government's lists.

We alienated our audience. We actually lost customers who had previously been perfectly happy with our service. Not one of my greatest triumphs in business, and a memory that still causes me to wake up occasionally at night with cold shivers...

Again, I mention the mistakes I have made in the hope that you don't have to go through the same process. We all make mistakes, and they only become stupid when we fail to learn from them. If you take one or two nuggets of advice from this chapter, I hope your marketing campaigns will be more successful than my irredeemable and poorly thought-out aspirin example.

John Wanamaker, a very successful US merchant and political figure who is considered by some to be a pioneer in marketing, is credited with coining the phrase 'Half the money I spend on advertising is wasted; the trouble is, I don't know which half.' That's food for thought for everyone involved in business, and a neat way of illustrating how concise your marketing campaigns need to be in order for them to be successful.

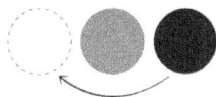

OUTPACING THE COMPETITION

"IF YOU DON'T HAVE A COMPETITIVE ADVANTAGE, DON'T COMPETE."

Jack Welch

You might assume that success in business comes because you are outstanding at what you do, but that's not true. It's really not that difficult; you just have to be better than your competitors.

You might be surprised to learn that business success has nothing whatsoever to do with being the best but everything to do with being better than the people that you're competing against. Of course, you might be both, but the standard of your offering actually doesn't matter in its own right. What matters is its relative merit compared to others in your market. It's not quite true that business is a zero-sum game, but in a field of winners and losers, you simply need to beat the competition.

UPDATED DATA

So at least help yourself out and study your competition. You can't stay ahead of people whose service offerings you don't fully understand. It makes complete sense to analyse major competitors and disrupters on a regular basis if you want to stay ahead of them. In a perfect world, you need to keep leapfrogging them in terms of perceived value and quality.

This can be relatively straightforward, but you need to dig deep and understand exactly what they are doing and how they're doing it, so you can try to objectively ascertain whether you could make improvements. Don't be surprised to find that they're watching you watching them!

Some questions you may wish to ask yourself include:

- What's their service offering? How does it differ from yours? Are they doing something radically different? Do they offer a service that particularly appeals to the market?

- What's their pricing structure? What payment terms have they put in place? Do they have particularly flexible or helpful return policies?

- How much do they pay their employees? Do they have a particularly innovative salary structure, or do they offer any performance incentives to staff? What are their margins?

- What level of customer service do they deliver? How long do they take to answer the phone, an email or any other form of correspondence? Are they doing anything particularly innovative in customer service that makes them stand out from the crowd?

- Do you have all of their sales collateral? Is their website, marketing strategy or social media presence noticeably better than yours? Are their accounts available, so you can run a slide rule over their financials?

You may be able to think of other areas you can examine by asking further questions. Leave no stone unturned.

ANALYSING THE DATA

Once you have been through this process, you should have a decent raft of information about your competitors. Now comes the process of analysing it. In order to make this process easier, I normally separate information into three categories:

- What are they doing that is worse than us?

- What are they doing that is better and that we can learn from?

- In what areas are we roughly the same?

Once you've created these categories, it will become much easier to understand where your business can improve and where you're already doing an excellent job. It will also assist you in integrating new ideas and offerings, as opposed to simply copying what the others are doing. You can effectively exploit the gaps you find in their strategy and ensure that you're doing things better than them.

I would strongly urge you to build up a resource centre of all of the companies that operate in your space and research them thoroughly. Make the information available to the majority of your staff. This will enable you to brainstorm ways of making your company stand out against your rivals; it can also be used to ensure that you have a clear voice and unique brand in the marketplace.

WORKS BOTH WAYS

Rest assured, this isn't some sort of unfair advantage that you are gaining, as I can guarantee that some of your competition will be doing exactly the same analysis on you! You can also be certain that they will find gaps in what you are doing.

An excellent example of this comes from the airline industry. Carriers are perpetually changing their pricing and everything about the way they structure flights, in the hope of winning customers from their rivals. Think about how many different flights you encounter when you search online; clearly this is a hugely competitive business and, when you're in a competitive market, you cannot allow the grass to grow under your feet. It's a game of cat and mouse.

Airlines are super agile. They continually tweak their loyalty plans and reward strategies, commit to changes rapidly, and communicate clearly and quickly with their customers. The airline industry is rather like the start of a Formula One Grand Prix, with companies continually weaving around each other in the ongoing quest for a temporary advantage.

All businesses can learn from this. It is a skill in its own right to be properly prepared and fully informed on competitors, regardless of whether you're a huge enterprise or a small start-up.

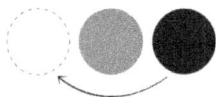

DO IT NOW

"YOU CAN DANCE IN THE STORM.
YOU DON'T HAVE TO WAIT FOR THE
RAIN TO STOP."

Vivian Greene

"THE WORLD IS TOO BIG FOR US. TOO
MUCH IS GOING ON: TOO MANY CRIMES,
TOO MUCH VIOLENCE AND TOO MUCH
EXCITEMENT. TRY AS YOU WILL, YOU
GET BEHIND IN THE RACE IN SPITE OF
YOURSELF. IT'S AN INCESSANT STRAIN
TO KEEP PACE… AND STILL, YOU LOSE
GROUND. SCIENCE EMPTIES ITS

DISCOVERIES ON YOU SO FAST THAT YOU STAGGER BENEATH THEM, IN HOPE-LESS BEWILDERMENT. THE POLITI-CAL WORLD IS NEWS SEEN SO RAPIDLY YOU'RE OUT OF BREATH KEEPING PACE WITH WHO'S IN AND WHO'S OUT. EVERY-THING IS HIGH PRESSURE. HUMAN NATURE CAN'T ENDURE MUCH MORE!"

The above quotation could be placed in almost any time period, and is certainly not out of place in the present day. It was, in fact, printed in the *Atlantic Journal* in June 1822 – a time and era that we would see as pedestrian compared with today. But the reality is that this applies to our time as well. One day, people will look back at the epoch in which we live and conclude that it was tame and uneventful.

MAKING BIG DECISIONS

The world may seem intimidating and making big decisions may seem overwhelming; there are always 100 valid reasons never to do something significant, to instead defer taking a risk. There is always comfort in the familiar and safety in the majority.

However:

"SOMETIMES YOU HAVE TO JUMP IN THE DEEP END WITH BOTH FEET, GET ON WITH IT AND SORT OUT THE CONSE-QUENCES LATER."

Gary Ashworth, 200 years after the Atlantic Journal article

Business is ultimately all about taking risks. If you're not willing to roll the dice, you definitely don't belong in the world of commerce. I have discussed this elsewhere in the book, but not everyone is suited to working as an entrepreneur or businessperson. Some people may prefer a more sedate pace of life, while others may favour specialising in a particular skill or discipline; it really depends on the individual. The Start section of the book is about reducing the odds of failure using the tips I've picked up along the way.

What is certain is that a sense of pace and urgency is an essential component of business success. These qualities should seep through every aspect of your organisation and be present in the ethos of your company as a whole. This concept is important both culturally and strategically. From a cultural perspective, it helps to ensure that people working for the organisation have the appropriate mentality. From a strategic perspective, it is important to understand that getting things done requires determination and drive.

BIG COMPANY PROBLEMS

The bigger the organisation, the more difficult it is to implement ideas and plans. Think of the innumerable layers of management and organisational structure involved in a massive corporation; ideas cannot turn into reality overnight if they must be filtered through this structure! By the time all the layers of managers and counter-managers have done their job on the liquid of commerce, you are left with heavily diluted coffee!

This means that ambitious projects depend on several key factors. They need to be extremely well thought out from day one, with plans that are costed thoroughly and implemented diligently. They also need a monomaniac in charge of the whole process, with an almost unholy dedication to ensuring that they are seen through to the bitter end!

Nonetheless, the old chestnut about prioritising what is important versus what is urgent still holds true. It's so easy to have our attention deflected away from what is critical, to the detriment of the business. Most of us spend our lives getting drawn into solving urgent issues, and these can become a quagmire that distracts us away from the really important tasks. Sometimes we find ourselves too busy fighting with bows and arrows to see the machine gun salesman!

WORKING CULTURE

In addition, many companies have a working culture that is far from helpful. The blame game is common in many businesses;

once this cements itself as part of the working culture, it is almost inevitable that procrastination paralyses any decision-making. No one wants to take responsibility or get into trouble if things go wrong, so everyone passes the buck and nothing ultimately gets done.

This is why it's so important to nip any negativity in the bud immediately and ensure that the culture of your company remains on the right track at all times. When you examine any successful person, you will almost inevitably discover that they have had a hugely positive mindset throughout their entire life. This applies equally to businesses and, while it is possible to soldier on through the negativity, no company will ever fire on all of its cylinders without adopting a positive and supportive mindset.

When procrastination becomes a part of the corporate culture, individuals, teams, divisions, companies and even entire countries face massive problems. This can be hugely damaging, so it is something to be avoided within your company. You must insist that your business perpetuates a culture that communicates both good and bad news immediately. Failure to do this will result in serious consequences and possibly even the liquidation of the company.

Top down

As with so many aspects of business, the culture is set from the very top of the organisation. Staff constantly look for guidance from top managers, so it is imperative that a culture of cutting through red tape and getting things done cascades down through the organisation like a virtuous waterfall.

There are many different approaches to achieving this, but Agile coaching has become particularly popular over the last decade or so. It has become a benchmark ensuring that companies work faster and more efficiently, which is becoming ever more important in the contemporary marketplace.

Ultimately, though, the only thing that keeps us going in business is the extra mile required to delight our customers; achieving this exalted goal involves fixing things quickly when they go wrong, often empowering frontline staff with the decision-making capability and budget to put things right immediately when the business veers off course. This will then find favour with our customers, who will acknowledge and appreciate our dedication to solving problems as quickly as possible.

Word of mouth

It is surprising how quickly word of mouth about a positive working culture can circulate. Anecdotes of exceptional customer service and the inordinate lengths that individuals have gone to in order to solve problems can rapidly become part of a company's history and reputation.

These tales become repeated, exaggerated and embellished with each telling, reinforcing the message and enhancing the whole process. There are many urban legends from the world of business that aren't true at all. One of the most famous for me is the mythology that has been built up associating Coca-Cola with Christmas, including the claim that Santa wears red to endorse the Coke brand. This theory is almost entirely baseless, but it hasn't stopped Coca-Cola from exploiting it at every opportunity!

I can think of several examples where resolving an issue quickly has made a huge difference to a particular company. A few years ago, I was travelling in Washington DC and had paid in advance for a room at a conference hotel. As it turned out, I was late arriving and called ahead to let the hotel know I would be a late check-in.

When I arrived at the hotel – somewhat tired considering it was 10pm – things didn't exactly go according to plan initially. I was informed that, regrettably, the entire hotel was full, including all of the suites, and that a mistake had been made with my booking.

However, the company was willing to go the extra mile to ensure I was satisfied. The young gentleman on reception made a call to a completely unrelated hotel nearby, which was also full but had a suite available. He got me into this suite at no additional cost, arranged transport immediately and ensured that I was comfortable there until the following morning. I was then transferred back to the original hotel, using the same method of transportation.

Instant response

What was particularly impressive about the resolution of my hotel problem was that no checking up took place. This was only a junior member of staff, yet he had the wherewithal to fix the issue immediately. I will never forget this efficiency and commitment to customer satisfaction, and consequently I remain loyal to the Fairmount Hotel Group to this day. There is no doubt that the company has implemented a highly positive and enabling working culture and consequently deserves to be hugely successful.

As well as providing customer satisfaction, another advantage of this mindset is that great people want to work for go-ahead companies with can-do attitudes. Such people are inevitably in a hurry to reach their goals, so they don't want to hang around in a negative or obstructive business. If a positive and constructive working culture is built, growth inevitably comes more quickly, and therefore opportunities and promotions unfold for talented people. There also tends to be a greater variety of work and problem-solving, which only makes the daily grind more interesting. It's another example of a virtuous waterfall, which then reaps reward for a business.

Danger signs

If you see individual employees becoming irritable, finding it hard to concentrate, showing a lack of attention and just generally displaying emotional dissatisfaction, then something is going badly awry. This will manifest itself extremely quickly and so it should be one of the most noticeable signs that you are pushing people too hard.

There can be other less obvious physical manifestations of this as well. You may notice people arriving late on a regular basis or taking more time off than is usual, or the average number of sick days in the company may begin to increase. You may even encounter some unusual behavioural indicators, with people eating or drinking too much, possibly even drinking excessively or taking recreational drugs to nullify the stress of their working conditions. Looking after the mental health of all staff is a duty all progressive cultures will embrace, with access to confidential help used as routinely as milk at the coffee point.

The true skill of a leader is to handle people as though you are their personal trainer at the gym. You need to stretch people to ensure they make the absolute most of themselves and their talents. But you have to get the balance right. Injuring them will be completely counterproductive; if they encounter any sprains, bruises or mishaps along the way, nurse them back to health and ensure they have the time they need in order to return to the very top of their game.

Previous environments

Companies often have workers who have spent time in environments that tolerated slow work. This can impact on your company regardless of the employee's personal qualities. If you do encounter this issue, then it's a quick-fix opportunity to increase productivity and profits: the person either speeds up with your coaching or you replace them with someone capable of fitting more seamlessly into your working culture.

Many of the companies I've purchased and worked with over the years have been in the staffing sector and, although they are fundamentally in different sectors to some of the other companies I've worked with, they all have one thing in common: the levels of productivity within these companies and niches are not standardised. There are marked differences in people's perspective on what 'full speed ahead' should look like.

It may seem obvious, but working environments need to be fun and people need to feel valued. There can even be extremes within the same businesses. When I walk into a post office in central London, I pity the people who work there. It's absolute pandemonium! They do not have a minute to themselves for their entire working day. Visitors are wandering around all over the place, paying no attention to the systems of organisation, and it's quite clear that the post office is ultimately completely understaffed. Now compare that to the culture of a small village post office and you will soon see the difference. They are often at the centre of the community, noticing local issues and bringing them to the attention of authorities in time to stop more serious problems. When I encounter both places, I have always reflected on the injustice that people working in the two different types of post office are paid exactly the same wage!

Power of managers

You need to understand another important aspect of the working culture in your organisation: the power of managers. Working differences are defined and tolerated by managers, so it is vital to ensure that they are up to speed with your requirements.

The managers you employ are your communicators of standards, working culture and the ethos of the business, so you must ensure that they truly buy into what you're doing.

It must be said that it's not always easy to compare yourself with competitors. However, if you interview their staff, they will tell you what key performance measures are expected. These are critical aspects of any business that you intend to assess or purchase. The speed with which the engine is running and the examination of costs and ratios of revenue to profits are of critical importance, as they are usually the easiest things to fix, achieving the biggest changes in the shortest periods of time.

Identifying these game-changers is often the difference between success and failure in business and, when making such decisions, it always pays to do it right now, not tomorrow.

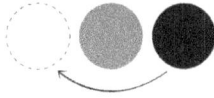

STAFF INCENTIVES: OWNERSHIP AND SHARE OPTIONS

"A SENSE OF OWNERSHIP IS THE MOST POWERFUL WEAPON A TEAM OR ORGANISATION CAN HAVE."

Pat Summitt

People value what they own. You only need to look at the way people behave in their own homes in order to realise this. Even the rowdiest and most slovenly teenagers suddenly become house-proud once they have acquired their own place. People never put their muddy feet on the chairs at home, yet often they don't display the same courtesy when they're sitting on the train.

In the world of business, sometimes you achieve your goals more easily and more quickly if you give part of the company away to a small but perfectly formed group of people with the talent and know-how to help you. Three quarters of an apple is worth more than no apple at all.

Having said that, it's not true in every case; it depends on the type of business you run. All sectors have their own dynamics. I can't see the value in sharing ownership in a manufacturing plant, beyond the chief executive, the finance director and the production manager, whereas in a recruitment business you might spread the ownership jam more thickly. There are some family businesses, dynasties even, who would be horrified by the idea of diluting their equity or having other shareholders questioning their authority.

Awarding share options, actual shares or other incentives at work is an art, not a science. My personal experience tells me that the trick is to give away just enough to attract and motivate key staff and make sure their terms are fair, but that in most circumstances you get the incentive back if they leave. I used to give a smaller amount of ownership to a greater group of people, as I thought my personal assistant would chew fewer pens if he or she had a small sliver of ownership. I was wrong. Spreading the jam more thinly resulted in the key people who could make the most difference not having enough to incentivise them properly.

Some of the giants, like Google and Microsoft, have created many millionaires by constantly giving out shares as part of the compensation package while the share price is rising, then buying them back and recycling them. It's one effective strategy for attracting and keeping rare talent in an extremely competitive market, where collective corporate progress leads to stratospheric valuations and share price growth. It doesn't necessarily suit us mere mortals.

I love working with people whose interests are aligned with mine. People who share the same passion go the extra mile; they are devastated when things go wrong and get excited when things go well. We're all prepared to do things you couldn't ask mere employees to do. We outperform. We're proud and aloof. We also celebrate together when we sell up; it's like we've all won the lottery.

Attracting and keeping top talent is important in virtually every sector of our lives, from the people who serve us coffee or sell us our cars and homes to the people investing in the digital economy we work in; from the doctors and nurses who fix us when we go wrong to the people inventing robots that we don't even know about yet to keep us company in our old age!

Some clever businesses manage to outsource aspects of their operations to others, but even those companies still rely on a few key people. If you're clever enough to have created a business where everything is outsourced – sales, production, delivery, accounts, marketing and legal – leaving you solely with a bank account in which people deposit money, you have my most sincere respect. You should be writing this book, and I should give up.

In my experience, even in times of high unemployment, there are always staff shortages in a raft of sectors, including new technologies and worthwhile jobs that don't pay well.

At the time of writing, there is still a hangover from Covid-19, when many people have spent time at home questioning and evaluating what they want to do. Many have decided to try something different entirely. Some have retired early. Some want to continue to work from home. Some may have had an epiphany and decided to leave the workplace and sit on top of a hill in a dinner jacket, learning the cello.

Meanwhile, business waits for no man. Demand for products and services chugs on, causing severe staff shortages and wage inflation. Even if everything we read about the automation of processes is true, and there's another industrial revolution resulting in millions of people losing jobs on a worldwide scale, it won't be any easier to find and keep the right ones: your A team.

TIE YOUR KEY STAFF IN

There's no right or wrong when it comes to awarding shares or share options. There are public company guidelines that used to recommend a maximum of 5% of the company shares under option over a 10-year period, to protect shareholders diluting, but I don't think the rule has been well thought through. The extra earnings per share created by motivated staff would outweigh any shareholder dilution.

In the people business I'm currently working in, we have incentivised the top team by giving them tax-efficient shares or share options that reward them with 20% of any upside in value created from the time they were gifted. That's about as generous as I would ever get. In this case, the business relies on talented people in order to grow at the rate we expect, and I'm happy to share 20% of the upside with my colleagues. Agreements are complicated and need to be drawn up by expert lawyers. Clauses need to be written to define good and bad leavers and, if there is no sale, in some cases a formula is agreed to buy back the shares at a theoretical company value.

The job market has changed over the last 10 years, and people stay in positions for shorter periods of time. There is little stigma attached to job-hopping. My father only had three jobs in his entire life, whereas nowadays if you are in a job for more than three years, you're likely to be asked if you're gathering dust. On the one hand, this means the labour market is considerably more unpredictable. However, it can also provide opportunities, if you get your house in order and work out how to recruit the top talent. We cannot be careless with our people, and we must never take them for granted.

BUILDING FOR A SALE

If you're not building the company for a sale, it begs the question: how valuable will your shares ever be and who will you sell them to? In these cases, share ownership might still tie people in, but there may need to be a mechanism for the shares to be sold and their value realised, possibly by the company itself buying them back in for cancellation. Alternatively, the company can hold them with a view to reissuing them to newly hired important people.

There are a lot of ideas and issues to think about in this chapter, but the message is simple. The cost of replacing staff is obscene. When you take into account the cost of hiring and onboarding someone new, possible recruitment agency fees, advertising costs and the time taken to select the best candidate, it is a massive undertaking.

You must hold on to your most valued and talented employees. In order to do this, they need to feel as though they own part of the company and will share in the success they are helping to create, beyond the reward of just their salary and a bonus.

My final tip is to make it fun. There's not much success where there's not much laughter. When your staff have a happy demeanour, you will know you're on the right track.

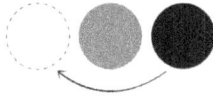

HOW TO MANAGE
DIFFICULT PEOPLE

**"MANAGE YOUR RELATIONSHIPS.
GREAT RELATIONSHIPS MAY NOT BE
PROFITABLE, BUT BAD ONES ALWAYS
RESULT IN LOSSES."**

Tarun Sharma

There are only three certain things in life: death, taxes, and encountering difficult people. However, we often don't merely encounter difficult people; we have to find a way to manage them.

We're all difficult people, though, aren't we? We all come packaged with our own odd characteristics. We all want to be validated, recognised, loved, included, promoted, praised; we all want to have a good moan sometimes.

In this post-Brexit, not-quite-through-Covid world, the workforce is restless. If you don't make your flock feel valued on a regular basis, the best sheep will be gone by the time you can say baa humbug. One thing is for certain, though: people change jobs more frequently in this new digital economy, and we can expect this process to be magnified in the current environment. In fact, according to figures compiled by the London School of Business and Finance, 47% of UK workers actively want to change careers[1]. There is also significantly less loyalty to brands or individuals in this environment, so the more that we can retain our existing talent pool, the easier it will be to grow our businesses.

There are staff shortages everywhere, and the war for talent is raging. Wage inflation is rife; in the businesses I've been involved with, salaries have risen by over 20% in many sectors. One US law firm, for example, is paying £140,000 starting salaries for juniors. Head-hunters are circling like vultures – I know this for certain, because I am one – and there's no longer any stigma attached to regular job-hopping.

However, because of this very candidate-led market, employers face a very demanding pool of talent, and this will undoubtedly mean working with and managing some difficult characters. So, how do you effectively manage those more troublesome individuals in the workplace?

Before we go any further, there are such things as hopeless cases. If you're stuck with racist, sexist or violent people, get rid of them. There is nothing you can do for them. If you attempt to sand down their rough edges, you run the risk of falling foul of employment legislation. It takes too long to change their behaviour, and your time is too precious. The good people in the workplace can easily become infected, as unreasonable people often try and persuade people to share their views.

NURTURE THEM

Train your staff well and help them reach their full potential. People are most loyal to the managers who keep developing them. Think of yourself as their personal trainer at the gym, pushing them to be the best they can be, giving them permission to be great. Understandably, people become irksome when they are badly managed, and are more likely to leave, seeking greener grass.

TREAT THEM WELL

Most people have left a job at some time in their careers simply because they were managed badly. Considering the time and expense associated with hiring, onboarding and training a new person, you should always look to keep your good people in place. In 2015, *Harvard Business Review* reported that the organisational costs of employee turnover range between 100 and 300% of the replaced employee's salary[2].

WORK THEM HARD

Workers become more difficult when they become bored in their roles. Their irritability can stem from being underworked. Don't be afraid to work them hard and showcase that you, as an employer, trust them and *want* them to rise to necessary challenges while stretching themselves and their abilities.

TACKLE ISSUES QUICKLY

Don't let staff problems fester. Disgruntled people look for others to moan to – and negativity is more infectious than the common cold, so it needs to be stamped out quickly. Prevention is better than cure, so ensure you have transparent communication channels and operate as much as possible with honesty and openness to nip issues in the bud before they grow into something bigger than they need to be.

CUT DOWN ON HOME WORKING

Home working can be the root cause of many employers' unconscious biases. Those employees who attend the office more often (and are therefore more 'visible') are more likely to get praise, form stronger interpersonal relationships with their managers and colleagues and, perhaps not intentionally, be the more likely candidates for promotion.

Additionally, home working is undoubtedly going to exacerbate gender inequality and negatively affect diversity and inclusion efforts. Those in care roles, traditionally women, may opt to work from home more often than their male counterparts in order to integrate domestic life more seamlessly with work life. They therefore risk becoming overlooked in the workplace due to a lack of visibility, and they will miss out on moving up the career ladder, widening the gender pay gap.

Avoid either of these problems as much as possible and ensure you create a level playing field for the *whole* team, who can then grow and strengthen as one unit without leaving anyone behind.

DON'T GET MAD

There's no place for anger in business, even when faced with the most challenging of behaviours. It's a sign of weakness. Remember that you don't have to be ruthless to be rigorous; you can still set performance standards and measure them without bullying. Rather than throwing your weight around, make it clear that your people are required to meet the expectations and ethos of the business, and then act when they fail to deliver. This will be far more effective than ranting and raving.

MEASURE THE SOFT STUFF

We talked about capturing and measuring data earlier in the book, but it's not just about the bottom line. The pulse of any business is always its people and, in fact, the best stethoscope to measure this can often be the consideration of soft factors. This doesn't mean becoming a practising psychologist or turning your business into a crèche! But it does mean paying heed to

> ## NOT ALL BAD BEHAVIOUR
>
> ## IS UNDERPINNED BY MALICE.

important human factors. Is there a sense of humour about the office? Is morale noticeably high or low? Do people have positive feelings about their working environment? Are they ultimately enjoying working for the company?

These are all key questions that managers need to be asking and addressing, if they have any pretence of running a successful business. It doesn't matter how profitable a company might be; if the staff are miserable, it will affect growth.

Fostering a positive mood among your workforce is critical. This can be achieved by concentrating on some relatively simple strategies and techniques. Seek feedback from your people and provide regular feedback yourself to managers within the business. Identify the trickiest employees and ensure that they feel valued, while also acquiring regular feedback from them. This is another way to ensure that they buy into the ethos of the company.

I've noticed that people who are apparently behaving outrageously often believe their conduct is completely reasonable. Not all bad behaviour is underpinned by malice. People frequently don't realise how destructive they are being and often you need to understand the underlying factors that have led to their conduct.

WEAK SIGNALS AND PRAISE

Troublesome staff can very much be compared to attention-seeking children. They start getting bored, become playful, and ultimately end up being disruptive if they don't understand the boundaries of acceptable behaviour. Luckily, though, they also tend to respond favourably to praise.

This means that it's critical to celebrate the success of all people within your business. Ironically, this is something that many managers fail to do adequately. Yet patting people on the back for a job they've done well can make a massive difference to their productivity going forward and can even affect their mindset about the company and their role within it. Sometimes, encouraging words can achieve as much as a salary increase, and neglecting this on a regular basis can be considered careless management.

Praise is free – and people love it! It could be argued that one of the consequences of our social media-driven culture is that people tend to crave recognition. This is a monster we have willingly created; it's a monster, though, that also represents an opportunity, as appropriately lavishing praise on staff members can do a tremendous amount for morale. There is no one happier than the staff member who feels valued, who is beaming with pride inside, and this person will rapidly become a highly productive worker.

DON'T FIX THE WRONG THING

Much of our work is based on self-reporting, and we know that marking one's own homework can be unreliable. We're rarely less accurate than when talking about ourselves!

To thicken the broth even further, this can work both ways. Some people are prone to what I call 'pro-noia'. It's a made-up word that means the opposite of paranoia. Many people I've worked with, especially in sales roles, are under the illusion that people are saying good things about them behind their backs, amplifying their achievements while significantly playing down their failings. They aren't. It's a fantasy. You may have noticed someone in the White House recently who was often prone to this...

Conversely, there are people with less confidence who mark themselves down. Perhaps they have a negative mindset and have a tendency to downplay their qualities and focus on what they perceive to be the weaker aspects of their personality or performance.

What this means is that staff often fail to articulate their challenges. Consequently, we don't address the real reasons that are holding them back. But with a little practice, we can teach ourselves to examine what's happening and not to jump in and fix the wrong things.

If one of our workers is failing, we need to think carefully about the reason why. We might assume it's lack of product knowledge, when really they don't believe in what they're doing. In this case, more training won't help. Their belief system needs boosting. Alternatively, it could be that their environment at home has become untenable, or they're going through a break-up. In this case, challenging their behaviour won't help. You need to get to the root cause of their particular issue. Everyone's different. Don't make the mistake of trying to fix the wrong thing.

EXPERIMENT LOTS AND KEEP WHAT WORKS

There isn't a one-size-fits-all approach; you're going to have to size people up. Sophisticated managers act as though they're making bespoke clothes in a Savile Row outfitter.

Different techniques work better with different people. Something that motivates one individual will have absolutely no impact on another – but that's absolutely nothing to worry about. We're all different. Some of us relish structure, some of us enjoy being creative, some of us favour sedentary tasks, and some of us can churn out number-crunching. There is no right or wrong, only different shades of humanity.

Modern management is about having the flexibility to add an individual element to the way that we manage people, while retaining a clearly defined framework of ethics and values. But within this framework, it's also important to acknowledge that human nature and instinct hasn't changed and isn't likely to change significantly in the future. Think of this approach as a more sophisticated version of the traditional carrot and stick.

KNOW YOUR LIMITS

Another aspect of our individual nature is that we all have different strengths and weaknesses. A person who appears to be a genius when conducting certain aspects of their work will not necessarily be well rounded in all facets. In fact, they may even fail miserably at other elements of their work. For example, some talented salespeople may win new clients with relative ease but may leave a wake of administrative disaster behind them wherever they go. You might be addressing this kind of issue continually and still experience absolutely no improvement whatsoever.

Society, and perhaps even human nature, encourages us to improve our weaknesses and view them as areas for development. I consider this to be backward thinking and ultimately counterproductive. After several decades of attempting to improve my own weaknesses, I don't mind admitting that I've given up completely. Instead, I focus on doing more of what I'm good at. This is considerably more liberating, far more productive and a key secret of all successful people.

If you experience a skills gap, don't try to become all things to all people; hire someone else to prop you up. This is why you should build teams with diverse and complementary skills in the first place, in order to ensure that every base is covered. Assemble a collection of players with different assets – doers, dreamers, optimists, soothsayers and moderators.

A racing team made up of brilliant drivers wouldn't even get the car built, never mind win the race.

DISGRACEFUL MANAGEMENT

Although in this book we're focusing on successful management, it won't come as an earth-shattering surprise to learn that many organisations tolerate dreadful layers of management. It won't come as a shock to many readers because they will have been on the receiving end of lazy, uncaring or biased management. They know that complaining about it won't help. Just the opposite: it'll be career limiting.

Some organisations are extremely fortunate and succeed despite (not because of) their management culture. We see high-profile examples of this being reported in the media on a regular basis. Many high-profile and well-known leaders engage in bullying or intentionally encourage a culture of fear and blame. It's an unnecessary barrier, though, and the consequences of bad management don't always become apparent for some time.

Narcissism is still rife in business. I'm perpetually surprised and horrified by the almost hypnotised state and blind faith that otherwise intelligent people develop. They invest in following atrocious leaders – people who have long since stopped taking advice from their peers before proceeding to lead their companies or countries into chaos and madness. This is all so avoidable, so I hope that at every level we can begin to make more rational management choices going forward.

WHAT ABOUT YOU?

Finally, it's important to remember that most of us have been troublesome at some point or another (I know I have!). If we reflect on our working careers, it's usually possible to identify a time when we were difficult to manage. There may be times when we've felt out of our depth and should have asked for help but didn't.

"

YOU MAY THINK YOU'RE AN

IMPORTANT BUSINESSPERSON, BUT

IT'S MORE IMPORTANT NOWADAYS

TO BE A COMPETENT SHEPHERD.

"

There is a phrase used in the business community: 'Communication is only as good as the response you get'. If you're not receiving the desired response from someone you're communicating with, you can reasonably conclude that it's you who are at fault, not them. It's advice worth heeding.

Equally, it is important to remember that all companies need behavioural standards. All unacceptable conduct needs to have consequences. The best way to deal with people is to isolate any problems, work with them to correct the issue, and assiduously measure their progress. Ensure that they receive rewards if they're doing well, but make sure there's nowhere to hide if they are doing badly.

Be patient and forgiving; lead your flock well but keep them in check.

You may think you're an important businessperson, but it's more important nowadays to be a competent shepherd.

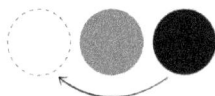

CAN YOU TRUST
THE BANK?

**"I THINK BANKERS WILL ALWAYS GET
AWAY WITH WHATEVER THEY CAN
GET AWAY WITH."**

John le Carré

Money makes the world go round, and banks remain the primary suppliers of this critical commodity in practical terms. Banking has always been at the heart of the capitalist system, and every entrepreneur will be reliant on the banking system in order to progress. Aside from a bank account, most businesses will have a line of credit in the form of loans, mortgages, leasing agreements or invoice discounting. Finance is central to the whole process of running a business, and borrowing comes in many different shapes and sizes.

Banks have had a lot of bad press in recent years, particularly since the 2008–2012 global financial crisis. Some might say, deservedly so – but the fact remains that your relationship with your bank is of imperative importance to your success as an entrepreneur. If you're going to succeed in any venture, it is essential to realise that banks are not like us.

Traditionally, bank managers have long been seen as pillars of society. However, it's important to be aware that they have a different outlook to us. Their interests are not the same as yours and mine. Running a growing company requires an entrepreneurial approach, which is fundamentally founded on taking risks. Banks are the complete opposite of this. From their perspective, failing to hit sales and profit forecasts or trying something that doesn't appear to work can be considered as failure.

While banking has diversified massively in recent years, with credit committees and computerised scoring becoming de rigueur, trust is still an important component of any relationship between a banker and a management team, and it isn't necessarily as easy to build as one might imagine. Bankers and entrepreneurs often find themselves creating friction due to their differing attitudes. Trust can take years to build, but it can be destroyed by one bad incident.

Many entrepreneurs and salespeople have an innate positivity, which is required in order to succeed in their particular field.

You have to push through a lot of negatives, a lot of rejections, in order to keep going, so having a negative mindset or a personality that becomes despondent in the face of challenges is unhelpful for entrepreneurs. Businesspeople often aim for the stars and are happy if they reach the moon.

This philosophy doesn't apply to bankers! It is a massive mistake to ever give a bank any financial or sales target that you might not reach, or to provide them with an aspirational budget. If you fail to reach this exalted goal, the bank won't view it as a sign of ambition, but as an indication of failure. Instead of shooting for the stars, be absolutely realistic in your dealings with banks. Provide them with a budget and cash flow forecast that you know you can achieve, or else you will run the risk of your bankers being disappointed with your performance, and the bond of trust between you being stretched to breaking point.

Banking covenants are put in place to protect the bank's security; if they are breached, the financial penalties can be high. Sometimes they act like traffic wardens; as soon as your meter ticks over, they're the first to slap a ticket on you. However, the collaboration between government and banks during the Covid pandemic was sensible, with the government-secured Bounce Back Loan Scheme (BBLS) for small businesses and the Covid Business Interruption Loan Scheme (CBILS) for bigger businesses being administered quickly, given the circumstances, by corporate bankers. Covenants have been renegotiated, and although there have been some business failures, many more have been avoided through the common sense and leniency of bankers whose penalties have traditionally been draconian when things slip below agreed standards.

BANKS CAN BE INCONSISTENT

Despite their ability to compute data quickly and accurately, it's not always possible to prejudge how a bank might react to your plan and, given the power they have, this doesn't sit easy with most business folk. You can't rely on them to act in a certain way. They're unpredictable; apparently similar circumstances can produce absolutely different results when dealing with different banks, people and even departments of the same bank.

An example that affected me personally was a situation where a business partner and I invested several million pounds in order to refinance a sizeable restaurant chain. This once successful business had fallen on hard times, but we believed that the core trade was exciting; the business offered healthy and voguish food that could succeed with the general public. It also had an excellent portfolio of locations, but the management team was weak and the financial controls flawed. Perhaps most seriously of all, they also owed several million pounds to banks, and this would never have been recovered had we not stepped in with a suitable rescue package.

In order to address the problems in the business, we quickly appointed a new chief executive and finance director with experience in the sector. I'll be honest, the following year was a struggle, but we slowly but surely brought the chain back to profitability, closing down some of the loss-making shops, permanently shuttering the head office, ridding ourselves of a debilitating lease, and cutting costs wherever possible. This pragmatic approach was ultimately successful, and we even won an award for a new flagship restaurant that we opened in central London.

So far so good, we thought. Other shareholders and our peers were impressed and enamoured with our progress, but the bank didn't quite see things that way. Because of the chequered history of the business, the relationship we had with our bank at the time was always strained in nature. This was difficult to turn around, since the company had already blotted its copybook several times in the past thanks to a catalogue of missed targets, profit warnings and false promises.

We soldiered on diligently, managing to reduce the amount owed to the bank by £4m over an 18-month period, but although progress had been made to a certain extent, we still faced frequent challenges. We were constantly in breach of our banking covenants, which had been harshly drawn up, given the previous conduct of the business.

The progress wasn't enough for the bankers. As soon as they thought it was feasible to sell the business for more than the amount they were owed, they instructed a firm of accountants to write an expensive report on its viability (at great expense to the company) before sending a demand for the immediate repayment of the balance. When we couldn't pay it, they appointed receivers to put the business into administration, as we had breached the loan terms. They unceremoniously threw us onto the rocks, leaving us to drown. We lost all of our investment, and so did all the other shareholders. The bank got all of its money back when the administrator sold the business to a third party, so the bankers were ultimately happy with the outcome.

I still wake up in the night sometimes with the cold shivers, recalling the nightmare of that period. I have a strong feeling that, had we not paid off the majority of the outstanding bank loan, the company would have pulled through and eventually become successful. But I forgot one of the key lessons for any business: if you owe the bank a small amount of money, you're potentially in trouble, but if you owe them an enormous amount of money, then they are the one with the problem.

DON'T PUT ALL YOUR EGGS IN ONE BASKET

Spread the risk. Have more than one bank involved in your business, if possible, then if one wheel falls off the wagon it won't bring down the whole train. When relationships go well, banks will often encourage you to have all of your accounts and sometimes your personal mortgage with them, keeping all the security in one place.

This is fine when things are going well, but awkward and inadvisable when markets tighten. Banks are an important business partner, but they are not family. It's better to have a variety of lending sources. Banks will tell you that they won't treat you as a singular financial entity – but, in my experience, they usually do. I once had some investment property and my business and personal finances all held with one high-street clearing bank, at a time when the property market experienced a correction. Suddenly, despite their previous assurances, my overall accountability was being questioned.

I was advised to sell the property and reduce the debt, even though it was at the low point of the property market. It was exactly the wrong thing to do, and I managed to resist the pressure, but it would have been easier if all my finances had been separate and no cross-guarantees had been given.

STICK TO THEIR KNITTING

It's also important to choose banks that specialise in the particular issues you are facing. They are experts in sectors and products, and you will be well advised to take advantage of these specialities. Some may favour retailers, others may prefer business services, and some lenders will specialise in the aircraft industry, or leveraged finance for acquisitions and asset lending.

Banks are generally not independent, and their staff will sometimes thrust uncompetitive products down your throat because it's linked to their bonus. Banks are experts in banking, just as you are an expert at running your business; it's important to become competent in what they offer so that you can negotiate with them effectively. Don't buy any magic beans, hoping they will grow into a beanstalk.

Banks are clever at writing agreements. It's their core business, and it's easy to be manipulated if you don't know what you're doing. Banks will try to get away with whatever they can. Fees can vary enormously, and charges can be disguised quite skilfully; some banks might charge an arrangement fee upfront, while others may build charges into the agreement along the way. Early redemption fees are commonplace and can vary enormously from bank to bank, and rates can often be repriced with little notice. Due diligence and legal fees are all payable by you.

Interest rates can be fixed or variable, linked to various indices or can even change as profit-to-debt ratios evolve.

TROUBLED TIMES MEAN A REGULAR FLOW OF INFORMATION

Don't keep secrets from the bank; it's a massive mistake. This might seem counterintuitive, but don't send financial statements late or dress them up. Take the bull by the horns and talk to your lender early.

Firstly, it's about trust. Even in an age where all projections can be modelled, a reasonable bank manager needs to look you in the eye and be convinced by your honesty; they need to have confidence and belief in your ability to fix things.

Secondly, have a plan that makes sense and will stand up to scrutiny. Cut costs where you can; you're certain of the savings if you do that, whereas even revised sales targets aren't guaranteed to materialise.

Thirdly, give the bank as much time as you can before you run out of cash. Banks need time to check your figures and get plans agreed by credit departments. If there isn't enough time, then the answer is no.

If you do ever require the support of the bank, you really do need them to be involved and invested in the turnaround process. They should be involved, sometimes on a daily basis, to ensure that they're part of something they helped to design. This means fostering and nurturing a strong relationship with your bank from day one.

Banks work with facts. Get all agreements in writing so that there's certainty from both sides.

KNOW YOUR BANKER'S LIMITS

It's useful (but not always possible) to find out the lending limits of your bank manager. This will help define the parameters of your business and its potential for capital, while helping both parties understand them as well. It's not unusual that they will be too proud or secretive to tell you, but it is useful to know whether they can make a decision without it having to be signed off by someone else. This can then help your negotiation with the bank going forward.

PUT YOUR ACCOUNT OUT TO TENDER

It's worth putting your accounts out to tender periodically to keep your bank honest, or you might find yourself overpaying.

It's not about the cheapest option, though. A banking relationship is a complex mix of criteria. If you can find a bank with whom you have a strong relationship that works, you should hold on to it tightly with both arms, even if you're paying slightly over the odds. Lending outcomes aren't decided by credit scoring alone. The business case and the people involved count too.

TIMING

We talked about giving the bank enough time in periods of difficulty but, as a rule, you need to give them more time than you think they'll need. Most banks I have dealt with have been sensible in their approach – but don't expect them to respond quickly to any lending process. If you think you might need to increase your line of credit, or renegotiate an existing one, don't rush them. They march to the beat of their own drum and have three speeds: dead slow, stop and reverse.

TRY OTHER SOURCES

With this in mind, it's always worthwhile to investigate other sources of funding. Banks will usually lend you money if you've got plenty of security to cover the loans. This means that if it's possible to borrow money from family, friends or angel investors, instead of risking all your savings, you will effectively be mitigating your risk. You don't want to be so concerned about this issue that you're like a rabbit caught in headlights – frightened to make the right decision for your company for fear of upsetting the bank.

CONSIDER ALTERNATIVES

Finally, you should always consider all possible alternatives for your lending and banking. One of the benefits of the globalised and online culture is that banking is becoming more diversified and cross-border, so you should take advantage of this. Consider lending sources from different continents and diverse sources.

Online banks have developed sophisticated products, and there is a growing market for crowdfunding. This has the advantage of not only publicising your business, but also potentially raising significant sums of money, and it also presents you with a ready-made customer base, one that is eager to consume your goods and services. You already have a fan club before you get started!

Mezzanine finance, venture capital partners and private equity companies can also be considered for bigger deals, but they can be expensive for core lending. It's common for them to charge rolled up interest, and they often require equity and charge board fees for their executives to work with you. If they have experience or contacts to bring to the table, or can open up new territories for your business, that's fantastic. But if they are only there to protect their investment, it can be an expensive and intrusive relationship, which might be difficult to curtail.

SUMMARY

Treat your bank with respect and care, just as you would any other partner. Get to know them, be honest, build up trust and keep them informed. Understand that they have a different way of working to your business and may view the entire enterprise from a different perspective. Banks are the oil that helps the engine run smoothly, and they might just be the facilitators of a prosperous and profitable future. However, you should treat them with respect, because the party stops when they withdraw their support.

Over my years in business, I have grown to appreciate, respect and love bankers. But I couldn't eat a whole one!

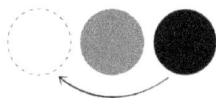

TENACITY AND EXECUTION

"IF YOU FIND YOURSELF WALKING THROUGH HELL, KEEP GOING."

Winston Churchill

Tenacity is the most important quality an entrepreneur needs in order to be successful.

No matter how well we prepare, it is inevitable that we will encounter hurdles in life, and sometimes crashing through these barriers requires an approach that is less than tentative. Passion is the oil that gets the engine running and helps us to break down these pesky obstacles. When you enjoy your daily work, the challenges you encounter on a regular basis become part of life's rich tapestry, rather than an insurmountable obstacle. The tenacious entrepreneur is able to take everything in their stride, and relish some of the challenges they must inevitably deal with.

EXECUTION VERSUS IDEAS

In my experience, how you execute an idea is considerably more important than the idea itself. There are hundreds of ideas circling around in life. You can find them on every street corner. They're debated in every pub. Some of them are brilliant and some are doomed to failure, but while there is no doubt that ideas are important, it is the way these ideas are put into practice that is ultimately the difference between success and failure.

If you simply do a good job in the business you set up, you'll make a living. Stick to business models that have been proven to be successful and you will ultimately do an outstanding job, and the world will be a richer and more rewarding place. This applies across all sectors, industries and livelihoods. If you're a plumber, turn up on time. If you're a builder, do the job on budget. If you run a delivery firm, tell your customers if things get broken. If you're a doctor, wait more than 20 seconds before interrupting your patient to give them the answer to the 'What seems to be the problem?' question.

There is no qualification, no college degree, no amount of intellectual ability that compensates for just caring about your customers. Walk a minute in their shoes and imagine, just for a moment, how they perceive you and how you would feel if you were on the receiving end of your service. Talent, genius and intelligence are an advantage, but not strictly necessary. They are no substitute for the power of focus and commitment. Every teenager understands the power of focus; just watch them set light to a piece of paper with a magnifying glass and a bit of sunshine. We're surrounded by magic and opportunity. We just need to find the courage to reach out and grasp it.

CONCENTRATION AND SUCCESS

Concentrating on the task in hand and putting in continued effort on a daily basis can help us all achieve the dizzying heights of success that many would consider inconceivable. Day-by-day progress, little by little. As they say: success by the yard is hard – but by the inch, it's a cinch. Even the least talented of us can be successful with a little application combined with some discipline and the belief that we can succeed whatever the odds. If you don't believe me, look at Donald Trump. If he can ascend to those heights, there's hope for all of us.

Tenacity is a critical component of any successful person, and it really just involves keeping going when others give up. It requires us to put up with short-term discomfort, tolerating challenges that require effort or fortitude, and pushing through in the pursuit of a higher goal. Determination becomes a habit. You can train yourself to be determined just as easily as you can train yourself to give up. You must master this personal quality and find a way to incorporate it into the culture of your company.

The message you deliver to staff should be that life, success and personal fulfilment are all a mind game.

In common with goal setting and reaching any targets, you need to break everything into bite-sized chunks in order to fool your thinking. If your brain contemplates a huge task all at once, the sheer enormity of it all can be intimidating. This can easily become a demotivating factor, which will significantly diminish our chances of completing tasks we don't enjoy – and, ultimately, our chances of becoming successful. All the time, I hear people telling me how proud they are to feel 'the burn' when they're exercising. It makes them feel good and they know progress is being made. The same discipline is required in business. Before long, you'll start to love it. That's something you can control.

CHUNKING FOR THE WIN

By 'chunking', you create tasks that can be completed within a relatively short period of time, and each one of these feels like a minor victory. It's the consistency that's effective – doing a little bit every day, every week, every month, rather than attempting to construct the Roman Empire in 24 hours. Chunking is a thread throughout this book and it's a technique that I believe to be particularly important and valuable.

Let me give you an example. There have been thousands of books written about dieting, and I must confess that I've purchased far too many of them myself! Diet and weight loss have grown to be a $71bn industry, yet, according to a study by Cora J Wilen, 95% of dieters regain their lost weight between one to five years[3]. This lack of success is all too regularly blamed on the diets themselves but, while this theory is not completely unfounded, the reality is that failure is usually due to the approach of the individual.

People who have lost weight haven't done so by magic. It's a slow grind, with one primary underlying rule: the rule of calorie deficit. Controversially, the Journal of the American Medical Association published a patient handout entitled *Healthy Weight Loss* in which the first sentence states 'a total of 3,500 calories equals one pound of body fat'[4]. This means it is perfectly feasible to lose a pound during the average week and to then repeat the process over and over again. If you stick to this plan, week in, week out, it's perfectly possible to lose three and a half stone (22.5 kg) in a year. This sounds like a vast amount and an incredible outcome, but it is actually achieved by following that basic approach and grinding it out day after day after day.

The reason why I've used weight as an example is that I've struggled to control my own weight for many years. I failed many times, over many years, before eventually finding a way to lose the excess 70 lb I had been carrying, and reaching my target weight. It was one of the most difficult things I have ever done. More difficult than much of the business success I have achieved. I wobbled many times along the way. I had setbacks, felt demoralised, felt like giving up. I sought help from others, joined slimming groups. I lost belief in myself. Found it again. I used whatever tools I could find to help me reach my target of 175 lb. Once I'd got there, I did indeed find that the rewards were worth the effort, and this has motivated me to stay there for the time being. The similarity to building a business is uncanny.

I've recognised that where I failed in the past with dieting is that I was unable to uphold the end goal in my head with enough belief to stop me from becoming distracted. After a certain period of time, I lost motivation. I no longer believed that the dietary programme was going to work and that my goal of looking different and being healthier would be achieved. Suddenly, my mind would switch; the mountain seemed too high to climb and the short-term pleasure derived from eating a cream cake seemed a more attractive option than grinding out a calorie-reduced diet for months on end.

Gleaming goal

That's why it's essential to enhance the image of the end goal. Make it bigger, brighter, louder and more exciting, in order to bolster your belief in the process. Make the journey fun, too. Involve other people and celebrate, with rewards for achieving the milestones along the way. Being in business can be lonely, and most of the burden is carried on the owner's shoulders. Join groups of like-minded, non-competing business owners or attend conferences where ideas are shared, new techniques learned and best practice defined. I'm always pleasantly surprised by how other people's successful ideas can be adapted to fit businesses I'm involved with. I call it creative swiping.

Mental stamina can be learned and built, just as working out will increase the size of our physical muscles. The same also applies to impulse control. When you introduce discipline into your life, it vastly widens the parameters of your potential achievements; and when you finally get to the place you were aiming for from day one, the sense of achievement will not only sustain you going forward, but will make you realise when you take on new challenges that you can indeed succeed. You have strengthened your backbone and improved your character, literally building a better human being. If you believe you can, then you can.

LIFE LESSONS

These are important life lessons, and the good news is that it's easier to instil this sort of determination in a corporate environment than it is personally. There are a few reasons for this, but I mainly think it's because you have a whole team of people to help you and there are financial rewards in place to encourage the discipline needed to achieve the goals in the working world. When people are having their leisure time, they naturally tend to believe that they should be doing something fun – they're not necessarily ready to put the hard yards into making their personal life about unending discipline!

In the corporate environment, not only do people come up with a readiness to work, but the goals of an organisation are more straightforward and transparent. It stands to reason that if you stay the course longer than your competitors, you will have a competitive advantage.

Properly motivated, most people want to do challenging jobs. They want to feel that they're achieving, they want to feel that they're making progress, they want to feel that they're growing in that working role. Of course, this doesn't apply to everyone. You will always get a few people who are happy to drag their feet and coast, but if you can spend time designing a culture in which you can encourage as many people as possible to look towards reaching their next goal, then success will become routine. In fact, to outsiders, it will just become 'the way we do things around here'.

BUILDING TENACITY

So, building tenacity in business is about setting the standards that you desire, measuring them effectively and revving the engine at a consistent, exciting pace without burning people out. Any company that intends to grow faster or achieve ultimate success learns to enjoy the slight pain that results from this process. That is because the goals are worth the effort. It's the glory of hard work. In her book *Grit – Why Passion and Resilience Are the Secrets to Success*, the psychologist Angela Duckworth argues that a person's level of stick-to-itiveness is directly related to their level of success and that it's more important than either talent or hard work.

Getting things done, though, is a different thing entirely. It's not just about fortitude; it requires a more structured and systematic approach. Completing tasks is about following through with well-constructed and properly conceived plans that cut through the hubbub we surround ourselves with in everyday life.

BOARD MEETINGS

Central to the process of creating adequate execution is holding regular board meetings to review progress. These meetings, attended by a properly composed board, are when the homework gets marked, triumphs are celebrated, problems debated, and the strategy can be tweaked going forward if necessary. The top team meet to review any progress, make decisions about the future, and shape the direction of your commercial enterprise.

Running a meeting might seem a straightforward task – child's play to an experienced organisation – but there are good routines that work well, and other routines that can be unhelpful or destructive.

Structured agenda

The key to these meetings is that they are based around a structured agenda, one that follows the same pattern every month. There is no point in having a higgledy-piggledy approach, as this will lead to disorganisation, confusion and ultimately poor decision-making.

It's vital that notes are taken which accurately reflect what's debated. These minutes need to have an independence or distance that allows them to appropriately reflect the discussion that has taken place, along with a list of action points that will be circulated ahead of any future meetings. It is also usual to distribute an information pack among all members at least 48 hours ahead of the meeting; this contains management accounts, cash flow forecasts and any other key metrics that you use to monitor progress compared with your budget.

The Companies Act and the articles of your company will drive what's required by law, but every meeting must start by confirming that a quorum is present (the minimum amount of people attending to make it official), and then the minutes of the previous meeting must be approved in order to ensure consistency across the organisation. This discipline is not only helpful for the goals of the business, but also contributes to creating a healthy working culture; people know there will be transparency and that their words will be taken seriously and recorded.

All this takes place before you even reach the agenda. It underlines the importance of prudently investing in a mature approach to meetings. Time needs to be spent running through the action points, checking that they have been completed in the time allocated or that the right amount of progress has been made.

Executives and accountability

Holding people accountable is a critical aspect of any meeting procedure, but can be a massive stumbling block for many businesses. There's a good reason for this: many high-status people are not comfortable being held to account, especially if they have powerful jobs and significant equity holdings. This is fine if you own the business outright – you can do as you please – but if there are outside shareholders, the job of the board as a whole and especially the duty of the independent directors is to make sure that these shareholders' minority interests are respected and not trampled over. Chief executives often have strong personalities and are used to getting their own way. Some surround themselves with sycophants, 'yes men and women' who will do as they command. These people aren't strong; they're bullies. Stronger people welcome the benefit of awkward conversations and honest feedback because they realise that uncomfortable truths need to be told and that airing them will help the company to progress.

Speaking about this topic reminds me of an awkward experience I once had. I was involved with a business that had been among the fastest growing in the United States. It was run by a particularly charismatic leader who needed some assistance after the market in which the company was competing had become commoditised and increasingly competitive. Although management at the company had been weak, those in managerial positions were enthusiastic and financial control had been strong. However, the company needed a hand to get back on track. It shouldn't have been a particularly difficult job.

As the 'new boy', I didn't say anything when the action points were skipped over at my first meeting. I thought it was probably an oversight, but this impression quickly turned out to be a misconception. After the third meeting, it became apparent that there was a culture running indelibly through the business, like lettering through a stick of rock, where people talked a good story but weren't ever held to account. Deadlines were missed and people were forgiven for missing them. Timetables slid and there were no consequences when people failed to do what they had promised. It was a disaster. Nothing ever got done.

Each meeting was a whirlwind of well-intentioned enthusiasm and intelligent discussion about things that were never satisfactorily actioned. I felt I should intervene, and things got frosty when I insisted that meetings couldn't start until action points were discussed. It soon became apparent that nobody wanted to be held to account. They weren't prepared to take the medicine they needed and were unwilling to create a culture that would result in transparency and excellence. I was never fired, and there was no confrontation; I just stopped being invited to meetings, as was their way. Nothing ever changed, and the business chugged along, making a reasonable living for the owner until she retired. The lesson I learned was that some people don't want to be held to account and it's not my job to force them to do anything they don't want to do. I saw a business that never reached its full potential, but they only saw a happy clan of people who soldiered on.

RUNNING YOUR OWN BUSINESS

That's the beauty of running your own business: you can do what you like. You don't have to take anyone's advice. You don't have to grow profits. You might prefer a lifestyle business, where you seek two days a week of leisure time. You can make up your own rules and break them. Go on holiday whenever you want, take days off when you feel like it and set your own timetable. Be careful who you hand down this business to, though.

There's an old Chinese proverb which just rolls off the tongue: 富不过三代. The characters roughly translate as 'You can only keep wealth in a family for three generations'. Members of the first generation work hard and make sacrifices to build a great business and are prudent with their money. The second generation have a much easier life. They don't have to make sacrifices or work weekends. They become accustomed to the luxuries their parents provided and can be careless with money, but their elders still provide them with some values and guidance. However, the third generation expect the business and the money to always be there, because that's all they've ever known. They've probably been educated at an expensive private school, where they were encouraged to follow career paths like food critic, poet, tiger hunter, yoga retreat owner or politician – anything other than running the family business, which is of course beneath them.

According to the proverb, it's apathy that stops businesses passing beyond the third generation. Easy come, easy go. That's why we need to make tenacity, grit, determination and world-class execution the keystones of our companies.

Most of my working time now is spent boosting the belief systems of owners, measuring what success looks like against the plan we have made together, and dispensing enough enthusiasm to make the journey interesting. I encourage people to have fun and make money with integrity. It works.

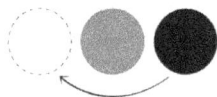

NON-EXECUTIVE DIRECTORS: YOUR SECRET WEAPON

"A NEDS ROLE IS TO MAKE SURE THAT THE MACHINE GUN SALESMAN ISN'T REJECTED DURING THE BOW-AND-ARROW BATTLE."

Adapted from a cartoon

'NED' is a slightly odd sounding acronym that may not be familiar to everyone; even when you know it stands for 'non-executive director', you may still be none the wiser. These part-time officers have the experience to turbocharge your business. For a fraction of the usual salary outlay, you receive a fraction of their time, but all of their experience – and the benefit of their successes, failures, lessons learned, battle scars and triumphs.

In fact, when they are used properly, having the right NED on your board can be a powerful secret weapon. Some of the compelling advantages of NEDs are not immediately apparent. That's why they deserve their own chapter.

UNIQUE RELATIONSHIP

Firstly, you don't have the same relationship with your NEDs that you do with other members of staff. Full-time employees will always be wary of telling you the truth, particularly when it's something you don't necessarily want to hear. This doesn't apply to NEDs. They are not full-time staff and so they will be far more willing to tell you the truth; they won't be overly concerned if this reality upsets you.

Going through this process isn't always a pleasant experience. We're all guilty sometimes of wanting to stick our heads in the sand, when often the painful truth is precisely what we need to hear. Life sometimes disguises our most valuable gifts as our worst nightmares but, by listening to the advice of outsiders, you can take advantage of their grey hair and wise words.

NEDs also won't take umbrage if they're fired, as they're not reliant on your company to pay their full-time salary. This means you're more likely to receive a balanced and nuanced view from your NEDs – unlike some of the other sycophants who work for your company, blowing smoke up your backside if you ask for their advice.

OUTSIDE WORLD

Another clear advantage of hiring NEDs is that their experience comes from the outside world. They have derived their talent working for other firms and have two advantages over internal personnel. Firstly, they bring external views in terms of best practice, with different types of strategy and problem-solving, which means they are able to view your company through a completely different lens. Sometimes, when you're slaving away on a daily basis, you can't see the wood for the trees. NEDs offer you a completely different perspective and this can be highly refreshing and insightful. Secondly, NEDs often have access to a raft of tried and tested competent experts they have worked with in the past. They will have a black book full of contacts that you can leverage.

It's important to use the limited time NEDs give to your business in the correct way. Don't waste their time by involving them in the day-to-day running of your business. Instead, involve them in challenges you haven't seen before and ask them questions you don't know the answers to. NEDs can be hired for any number of specialist skills – helping with an acquisition, implementing a new software system, or any other project you might have in mind. For companies with minority shareholders, having a NED to represent them can give reassurance that their voices are heard. Although a NED's pay might be modest, as an appointed officer of the company they have the same fiduciary responsibility as any other director to follow the law and the rules of the Companies Act. The same penalties apply if rules are breached. It's not unusual for big companies to have 10 or more NEDs, with different silos of skills and responsibilities, but most businesses I have been involved with have had an average of two.

RISK

Any potential NED worth their salt will be as cautious of joining your company as you are in your own vetting process of them, and they will conduct their own diligence into your company and track record. The legal responsibility that goes with the role will vary in significance and scope, depending on whether the company needs to be audited and whether it has external shareholders who will be reassured by the inclusion of an independent director on the board.

It's important to see things from the perspective of your NED as well. They do not want to damage their reputation by joining an unreputable company or be involved in any form of public crisis or criticism. The financial rewards they receive are nowhere near the risk involved, so you really need to make sure your house is in order and that all your processes are above board before you approach any candidates.

NEDs play a significant role in ensuring that the financial affairs of a company are honest, that processes related to the board are up to date and relevant, and that your overall operations comply with all the current regulations. It is common for NEDs to sit on audit and remuneration committees, ensuring that the benefit packages for senior executives are not completely out of kilter with market rates; in the process, they ensure that any outside shareholders are not disadvantaged. However, they are not going to be agreeable to this process if they feel their reputation will be significantly damaged.

Of course, if your company remains private, you can pay your executive team whatever you decide; that's the beauty of not having outside shareholders. However, even in this scenario, NEDs may have other roles.

PROJECT MANAGEMENT

Another way to utilise your NED is to give them overall responsibility to research any new internal or external projects. It's quite common for companies to require assistance with issues that are outside of their core skill areas. A distracted core business team can lead to a downturn in profits as eyes are taken off the ball, focusing on things they haven't experienced before.

That's when relying on the skills of your NED really comes into play. There can be several scenarios in which this occurs. It could be that your company is dressing itself up for sale, considering an important acquisition, implementing a new software system, floating on the stock market, or even delisting. For a variety of situations, NEDs can really help deal with these unfamiliar processes, leaving you to ensure that business is run as usual.

NEDs offer an end-to-end solution. Unlike external contractors, consultants and project managers, who leave when their work is done, NEDs stick around and ensure that everything is properly completed and functioning and that the overall process is successful. They may not be as committed as you are, but they do have a vested interest in the success of the company and won't just abandon a project when they feel they've done the minimum amount of work.

This is frequently reflected in the way that NEDs are paid, with companies often providing a small sliver of equity (not materially dilutive) in the form of options or warrants for their meaningful contribution, so that their interests are linked with the success of the company. However, this isn't the case with public companies, where rules don't allow it because it can be argued that such incentives, which are aligned to management goals, could compromise the NEDs' independence.

MY EXPERIENCE

I have worked in the role of a NED, so I do have some practical experience of this position. I've also declined positions where I didn't believe in the company or its leaders. One of my roles was working with a property business in Savannah, Georgia. The business and its owners knew much more than I did about local property development, sales prices and vacation rentals. I couldn't possibly have delivered anything of value in that area of the business, but my job was to help them secure financing and lock down their business model.

In this particular case, they were able to secure a 15% rental return on their assets, while taking the upside of the capital appreciation. We releveraged their portfolio with a local bank, agreeing a set of covenants that gave them enough headroom. This was very reassuring for the company, as it meant they didn't have to continually look over their shoulders, nor were they constantly worrying about being in breach of regulations.

In this case, my role ended after 18 months. By that time, they had learned everything they required, and the small investment I had made in the company when it was in start-up mode was repaid handsomely. Eventually, the partners went their separate ways, having profited to the tune of several million dollars each.

Raising capital

On another occasion, I was brought into a business to assist the senior management team with the raising of capital which would enable them to buy out the founder of the company, who had made the decision to retire from business. This sounded relatively straightforward on the surface, but it turned out to be a stretch to complete, and the solution that we finally put in place turned out to be a compromise for both sides.

Ultimately, we managed to raise a decent slug upfront in the form of senior debt, without making any personal guarantees, and then paid off the balance in full over a two-year period to the owner. It wasn't perfect, but the deal was completed and everyone got paid. Happy management team. Happy retired owner.

The correct use of a NED is a sweet help to the business and helps the wheels turn more easily. Having been involved in both the hiring and being hired part of this process, I've viewed the role from both sides. I've seen advantages and friction from all perspectives. NEDs provide the grit you need in the oyster. The right ones can be highly skilled individuals who bring a measure of independence to your business and deliver things that would otherwise be considerably more difficult to achieve.

TRACK RECORD

When hiring a NED, it's important to trawl through the market as you would with full-time staff and make sure you find someone with the appropriate track record and experience, as that's the only reason you're bringing them into the company. It's important to check up on backgrounds and to ensure that everything they claim to have done is true. Ask for recommendations, take references, speak to previous clients if you can.

In some cases, their work is done when the project is finished. Even if they are a business advisor helping the board along its merry way every month, NEDs can get stale and should be changed every few years, or at least reviewed in three-year tenure brackets.

To sum up, the advantages of bringing in NEDs are both tangible and numerous:

- They have the track record and experience that people within your company do not necessarily possess.

- They won't tell you what you want to hear; they'll tell you what you need to hear.

- They have an outside perspective of what best practice looks like and can provide a unique perspective on your company.

- They have a valuable network that offers value for your business.

- They keep the management team in check and are more interested in the processes involved with your business than outside contractors or consultants.

- They have an independent and objective view, while also being highly informed.

NEDs may not be known to everyone and may not be an option that all companies consider. But a high-functioning NED is the oil that helps the engine run smoothly, and the mechanic who knows what to do when there is an unexpected breakdown. No vehicle should be without one!

CONCLUSION

There's been a lot to think about in this section, because scaling up a business requires a different set of skills and a different mindset than starting one (in other words, what got us here won't necessarily get us there), which is why I've chunked down the chapters into bite-sized portions.

As a result of this, you should be writing a clear plan for the next 1,000 days, one that defines the roadmap from where the business is now to where it will be in the future.

You'll have been creative, thought about the risks and investment points, organised your funding and put in the correct measures and timetables to make sure the odds are tilted in your favour. I hope you'll have given some thought to whether you need a different board of Generals to help you along your way. In addition, you'll have decided the marketing and branding techniques you'll be using alongside your unique, hard-to-copy service or product offerings, which will enable you to outpace your competition with precision and gusto.

It sounds like a lot of work, but holding the end goal in your mind while breaking down the tasks into manageable portions will make it a much easier journey.

You are not in start-up mode anymore. Understandably, when you are in the early stages of your business, it can be easy to focus on the day-to-day, delivering work, pleasing clients, chasing new business, making sure staff are paid and generally doing whatever it takes to survive. You aren't that person anymore; you need to let go of that stuff and focus on the bigger vision. That is not to say those things aren't important but it's about building a team that takes care of those things for you so that you can push the business closer towards the end goal, the pudding. I want to help you draw your energy in that direction. For absolute clarity and a plan, you can trust and rely on, use my strategic business questions to recalibrate that vision, formulate what needs to be done (and by who) and the conversations that need to be had. You can get that at **www.garyashworth.com/eatthepuddingfirst**

Or if you are deadly serious about turning that vision into a reality, and you'd like to explore the possibility of me helping you then get in touch to see if we could be a fit at: **www.garyasheworth.com/contact**

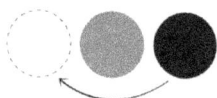

SELL

"WHEN THE TALENT IS TORRENTIAL,
THE HARVEST IS INEVITABLE."

Curtis Tyrone Jones

You only sell your business once – so after all the years of effort, worry and sleepless nights you've put in, you'd better get the highest price for it. That won't happen by accident, unless you're very lucky.

This was the goal you set at the beginning, and it's the culmination of all of your effort and enterprise from the day you started. All roads lead here. That's why you dreamed and planned to eat the pudding first!

Even if your goal isn't to sell to outsiders, but to create a family dynasty, careful planning will need to take place at the right time to hand over control, transfer shares and consider the tax implications. These are skills best left to professionals who can consider all options.

Yet statistics tell us that the majority of buyers are unhappy with what they have bought when they find that the hype doesn't live up to the reality. *Caveat emptor* – buyer beware.

It astonishes me how many companies fall at this last hurdle and sell too cheaply. They decide to sell at the wrong time in the cycle, or before the company has been groomed to get the best price. Often, the owners are convinced that a deal will go ahead before the ink is written on the contract and go along with last-minute price drops. We can't let that happen to you! Corporate finance houses are often selling distressed businesses that have run out of cash, lost key customers or where the shareholders have fallen out.

A business I looked at recently in the leisure sector was doing so well that it wanted to focus on growing its core business profits. The owners sold off a subsidiary, where they had spent £18m in the previous 12 months building a state-of-the-art factory, for a £4m sale price. They believed the subsidiary to be a distraction and just wanted a quick sale.

It takes preparation, planning and a proper strategy to achieve the outcome you want. Hiring a third-party broker to present

the business in the best light and negotiate on your behalf will normally result in the highest price, because they are experts in their field too. The right broker will adjust your earnings and take out any one-off, non-recurring costs or personal expenses that are not really business related.

But who should you choose? When should you engage with them, and what fee arrangement should you agree? How can you get multiple parties bidding against each other so that the price goes up?

In some cases, that means planning a year or more in advance. You may speed up or delay making investment decisions, reduce your cost base, trim any fat to maximise profits. You may groom a different management team to take over from you when you leave, or name a successor.

How do you know if the price is right, or whether it's the best time in the cycle to sell? We discuss many of these issues in this section because it's hard to get independent advice; asking many of these advisors if you should sell your business is like asking a hairdresser if you need a haircut. They all stand to earn substantial fees from the sale process, so you'd be wise to rely on the independent advice of one of your NEDs to help you. Hopefully, you'll have engaged one who has been through the process before.

When I came to sell Abacus Recruitment, it wasn't a simple task at all. I was in strange territory. I'd never sold a company before and needed a helping hand to agree fees and understand the process. Emotionally, I felt very vulnerable, too – when I needed to be at my most logical. It felt as though the piece of clay I had moulded into a living, breathing company with a personality of its own was being transferred to another owner.

I recognised that exact same feeling again later in life, when my children met partners of their own and left home to go and live with them. It was what I wanted, it was all part of the plan, but nevertheless, it still felt slightly unnatural and lonely. I realised that companies can be vulnerable to abuse by their new partners, just as young adults are. There's always a small part of you that wonders whether all parties are making the right choice.

That's why it's much easier to buy companies from corporates. They're much more matter-of-fact about things and you don't have to act as their counsellor as well as the buyer.

Abacus was a public company, so I had to digest the takeover code. I also had to make sure I could get over 90% of the shareholders to agree, which would mean we could squeeze out the remainder and deliver 100% of the company to the new owners.

We hired a broker that knew our sector, and they ran the sales process. We paid them a chunk of money upfront to 'write the book' (which presented the company, its people, its strategy and its profits in the best light) and agreed a percentage of the sale price if we achieved an agreed value, with a ratchet that paid them more money if they achieved a higher sum. Confidentiality was imperative, since any leaks could have affected the share price.

The company was going through a growth phase, so we were confident that we were leaving something on the table for the new owners to benefit from. After several conversations, we shook hands on a deal with a company that offered a good price and where we felt there was also a culture fit. Lawyers were engaged, while the buyer deployed a team of people to examine the business and report back. The costs started mounting up and up.

This is a dangerous time in the process – and canny buyers know that. In my head, I had already planned what to spend the money on. The deal was as good as done. My wife and I got excited about what we would do with the rest of our lives, the lifestyle we would lead and the financial security we had created for our children.

I was devastated when the buyer tried to change the deal. They said they couldn't raise the money and we would have to either take less or take some of their shares in exchange for ours. The deal fell apart and the fees were wasted.

I remember lying in bed staring at the ceiling all night, not being able to sleep for one moment. It was difficult to get up in the morning and start the process again. I was worried that new buyers might think we were tainted or that the original clowns had found something that had put them off.

Eventually, we found another suitor at the same price, and the deal was completed. I stayed on for a while to hand over to the new management team – and, during the process of reporting to a boss again after 15 years, I realised I was unemployable.

Since then, I've sold other businesses. The process always differs, but the emotions usually stay the same. You're giving your baby to someone else to look after forever.

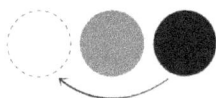

APOSTLES OR
TERRORISTS?

**"I WON'T COMPLAIN.
I JUST WON'T COME BACK."**

Half of all mankind

Have you done enough to keep your customers loyal?

It's an important but difficult question to ask. Most companies don't understand that being good, and even sometimes being great, isn't necessarily enough to keep your customers coming back for more.

It's only when customers are singing your praises from the rooftops, and would score you at least 9/10, that they will return regularly and recommend that their friends do the same. Word of mouth gets distorted, and stories of good and bad experiences are enhanced and exaggerated with every telling.

Unfortunately, the sort of blind loyalty we witness from football supporters doesn't apply in business. Customers are not like fans; they are prone to getting bored, wandering off, and ultimately abandoning you completely.

Feedback doesn't equal loyalty. I'm sure you've been to a restaurant where the manager has asked you to comment on your dining experience.

They may have asked:

- How was the food? – Great, thanks.

- Did you like the wine list? – It was spot on.

- How was the service? – Excellent.

The manager of this restaurant probably walked back to their office with a smile on their face. It is even possible that, in some progressive companies, their bonus might be linked to customer satisfaction.

However, although it appears that a good outcome has been achieved, the correct question wasn't asked. The correct question is: 'Have we done enough to keep you loyal?'

Despite a pleasant experience, the truth is that we might try somewhere else next time. The restaurant hadn't done enough for us to become apostles. The questions weren't linked to the outcome.

You can see where I'm going with this. It's not just restaurants that have to work extremely hard to earn this level of loyalty; it's the same with most businesses. It's only when you can really delight your customers that loyalty kicks in. Never mind being alright – even being good isn't enough.

So how do you go about achieving this?

EMPOWERING THE WORKERS

One way to inspire customer loyalty is to empower workers in the lower ranks of the business to fix problems beautifully before they get out of hand. I've seen many examples of this during my business career. I met a hotel manager in Singapore whose hotel won the prestigious award for the best luxury hotel in the world.

I was impressed and fascinated to understand how the hotel had achieved this outstanding level of customer service. When I queried this with the manager, he explained that a simple cultural shift was at the heart of the success. He had decreed that every staff member had to ask for the manager's permission before declining any request from a guest, no matter how unusual or bizarre it might be. This is a fascinating idea; it's something most hotels simply wouldn't consider, yet it was a shift that enabled this organisation to put the customer at the heart of its working culture. It truly embodies the ethos of the customer always being right.

That simple but important alteration in the hotel's cultural DNA led to immediate changes in staff behaviour at all levels, such that their default position was to be helpful at all times and in all situations. Naturally, this then had a massive knock-on effect on the level of customer service they delivered… and so this virtuous circle began which culminated in them receiving the enviable award. It was a brave move.

At the other end of the scale, it really doesn't take too much going wrong to infuriate customers. You can alienate customers with the most trivial mistakes, and once they have a negative impression of your brand, it is very difficult to reverse that feeling. We like to believe that we make rational decisions about things, but, in reality, most human beings are driven by emotion. Once they have a negative association with you, it is difficult to shift that impression. They become hostile.

EXAGGERATION

Once you have upset a customer, they will tend to embellish and exaggerate their experience, rather than giving you the benefit of the doubt. They will entertain their friends and colleagues with colourful, exaggerated stories about your incompetence and their misery. In relation to your business, they become terrorists, attacking your brand and creating chaos. They will take time out of their busy lives to write letters of complaint and bad reviews and to warn off anyone who will listen. It becomes personal. There are brands I won't shop at ever again because I've been annoyed by the way I've been treated.

I've seen disgruntled customers go further; in some extreme cases they will even set up their own websites, such as Britishairwayssucks.org or pissedconsumer.com, in order to encourage others to complain with them. We British enjoy a good moan so, before long and with the help of social media, thousands of people could have heard a story that only contains a grain of truth.

The damage to the image of your company can be immeasurable and irreversible, so going the extra mile to fix things quickly and beautifully at the time the problem happens can turn terrorists into apostles. That's because, when things went wrong, they tested you – and you listened, empathised, put things right and delighted them.

AIR MILES SCAM

I've mentioned the airline industry previously, but I cannot think of a better example of an industry full of companies that treat customers badly and upset them in the name of loyalty. This seems ironic, considering how much effort they put into their loyalty programmes, but still many carriers seem to think it is totally acceptable to mislead their customers and make it difficult to redeem rewards.

It's commonplace in the airline industry for carriers to advertise their glamorous loyalty schemes, with compelling photos of sun-drenched beaches and glittering promises of free flights to exotic destinations. But these can often be difficult to book, even assuming you're prepared to navigate a complicated website or wait on hold long enough to speak to someone. The experiences are elusive, which leads to resentment. It's as though the entire programme has been set up to disappoint customers.

Airlines haven't exactly been transparent. You're not made aware of how few flights qualify on a select list of routes. If you're lucky enough to wade through the terms and conditions and actually book something, you'll often find that the taxes and hidden fees don't reflect the promises offered by the advertising. Most air miles schemes have a shelf life and run out after a period of time, so they can dive down the tiers from hero to zero.

CREATING AN APOSTLE

I once went to Venice for a weekend with my wife, and her luggage didn't come off the conveyor belt at Marco Polo airport. Alitalia had lost it. However, they located the case, phoned to say it was on its way, then delivered it by boat to our hotel and hauled it up the stairs to our room.

My wife is now an advocate of that airline and will be for the rest of her life. They really can do no wrong in her eyes because they fixed their error so beautifully. Her loyalty to Alitalia has lasted significantly longer than our marriage did! However, this is an excellent example of how you can create a bond with a customer and then count on their patronage for the rest of your existence.

In a similar way, online companies quickly gain respect and garner customer trust due to the way that they make it easy to return goods and refund money. Now, I'm not advocating that we should deliberately offer our clients and customers a bad experience and then fix it beautifully, but the benefits of this do make you think…

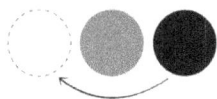

SELLING
A BUSINESS

"THE BEST THING ABOUT BEING RICH
IS THE FREEDOM. FREEDOM TO DO
WHATEVER YOU WANT, WHENEVER YOU
WANT. IT DOESN'T SUCK."

Tommy Lee

N o matter how passionate you may feel about a particular business or company, there comes a time when selling the enterprise is the only sensible decision. This may
be due to simple financial motivations, due to a change in life
circumstances, or because you find yourself wishing to move
into another field. Whatever the reason, selling a business is an

important part of any entrepreneur's journey, and it's a process that requires careful consideration and planning.

It's important to take all your people into consideration when selling any business. This is not just important from a moral and ethical perspective; it will also have a big impact on the practical success of the sale. If you're selling a business – particularly one based on customer service and people-facing activity – it is vitally important that you retain all staff and keep things as stable as possible. There will naturally be some discomfort among employees, but you won't have much of a deal in place if they all leave.

KEEP SCHTUM

It's very important to retain an overarching sense of discretion during the selling process. You shouldn't tell anyone anything in advance about the sale, as this can really prejudice the process. Rumours can circulate wildly, flustering the staff, causing uncertainty in the process and taking people's eyes off the prize. People start gossiping in corridors when they should be working.

Involve as few people as possible on a need-to-know basis. Only circulate details with your top management team and be obsessed with confidentiality at all times, so you can ensure that no private information circulates amongst the rank and file. If you do feel the need to talk to someone, take your dog for a walk.

ANALYSE YOUR REASONS

Selling your business is an emotional time when you need to be at your most logical, so you'll need to keep questioning and analysing yourself all the way through the process. Are you sure about the reasons why you are selling? Is it the right thing for you and for the business? Are you getting the best price? Is it a merger or an outright sale? Are you forming a partnership? Do you want to strategically strengthen the business? Will you be staying on after the sale and, if so, how will you feel about working for someone else? Is the buyer bringing something to the party apart from money? Are there cross-selling opportunities post-deal? How important is the best price? Is that your only factor?

Clear answers to these questions will help you through the madness of the sales process, as they will guide your true wishes. It's like a wedding; you can change your mind, although there may be consequences and fees payable. You can still say no right up until the time you're at the altar signing the sale and purchase agreement.

HIRE BAD GUYS

Dealing with any sale can be a messy business; that's why it is advisable to bring in some experienced muscle to deal with the process. It's a good idea to use a broker or a corporate finance house to present your company in the best light, find suitors and negotiate the best price. Professional buyers take a tough stance during negotiations or drop the price right at the end when you've mentally checked out. Although it's difficult to avoid, don't dare to dream how your life will change or discuss any of the exciting things you might do with the money until the ink is on the paper. It'll make you more likely to cave in if the price is chipped away at as you approach the finishing line.

You may well end up working with the acquirer of the business after the process is over, particularly in an 'earn-out' situation, so it's vital that someone else acts as the bad guy to keep the relationship between the principals civil throughout. Your buyers will also respect you as a formidable operator and nobody's fool rather than a doormat to be taken advantage of.

GET GOOD TAX ADVICE

Obtain some good tax advice well in advance. Tax can be complicated, and it only takes one mistake for you to fall foul of the taxman. It may take months to put in place the correct structuring so you can maximise the reward for your efforts within the legal confines of the tax system.

Now's the time to pay experts to spell out the tax implications and timing of payments. You should take time to understand all the elements of the deal yourself. Retirement relief, reinvestment rules, rollover relief and capital gains tax may feature and have an impact on the way you structure a sale. It is common practice for tax clearance with government departments to be obtained in writing before completion, so put in any application well ahead of time if you don't want to delay things.

FIX FEES

When you're selling a business, there will be many intermediaries to pay as part of the process; it's just a necessary part of doing a deal. Accountants, brokers, PR experts, tax specialists and lawyers love to charge for their services on an hourly basis, and fees can run away with themselves during lengthy or contentious negotiations.

Most of these people, though they may not like it, will work on a fixed fee basis if you push them hard enough. If they won't, then hire one that will. Ideally, you'll want to agree a fee that is contingent on the successful completion of the deal, with a smaller abort fee payable if things fall apart.

Now is not the time to be sentimental. Don't be tempted to use your existing lawyers and accountants to do the work if they aren't qualified. I'm a great fan of loyalty, and some of these professionals might see it as their last payday before you go, but you usually only sell your company once and you need to feel secure in the competence of a specialised, experienced team. Even when you agree fixed fees in writing, your advisors will often ask for more when the deal is done. I can't tell you the number of times that I've heard them whine on about 'how much they've got on the clock' and 'how much they're going to have to write off'. Resist their pleas and tell them just to bill you the agreed amount. Be aware that some costs will be for you to pay personally, since you are the client, and so will not be charged to the company.

TEAMWORK PAYS

Teamwork pays in most aspects of commerce, and selling a business is no exception. Your management team will be crucial during the sales process, so it is important that you assemble a competent group of people who gel as a collective. You'll be spending a lot of time together.

Not only will this help the process, but the company will be worth more if you're not perceived as being dependent on too few individuals. Potential buyers will be able to observe the inherent value of the company if you are able to conduct business in the usual fashion, despite being distracted by the sales process.

REVEAL THE FACTS

Honesty and transparency are important from the start. Any buyer worth their salt will conduct financial, commercial and legal due diligence thoroughly.

Although you want to present your company in the best light, you shouldn't hide details of poor debtors, security of contracts, and so on. Be upfront. Inconsistencies will come to light during this discovery, and a buyer may use this information to chip away at the price. It's quite usual and part of the negotiation for all the shareholders of a private company to sign several pages of warranties, swearing that they have disclosed all they know. Forgetting to mention something may result in financial claims and penalties.

It's important to remember that any purchaser is not expecting perfection – just an honest appraisal of authentic facts. Giving people a true impression of the overall state of the business saves time and reinforces good will. Ultimately, it's common sense.

GET REFERENCES

Many buyers will make an initial offer for a business that is high enough to knock other bidders out of the process, only to find reason to drop the price once due diligence has been completed. In a similar way, you might accept a high bid for your house, only to be presented with a reduction once the survey has been done.

If it's possible, take references from previous deals your acquirer has done, in order to discover how honourable they have been on previous occasions. You need to know who you're dealing with. It might make a difference to the bid you accept.

FORGET THE FAT LADY

While we're all in the process of selling our businesses and getting excited about the cash we are set to receive, it's important to keep in mind that the procedure doesn't end with this transaction. The tax and commercial warranties you sign may last for several years, and claims can be made if the information provided wasn't accurate or, in the worst-case scenarios, has caused loss to the acquirer.

What I'm saying is, don't spend the lot at once. Put a bit aside. Be a little bit conservative. Depending on who you sell to – and how the business performs – some of these warranties may be claimable, and you don't want to leave yourself in a position where you might not be able to meet any liabilities that might arise.

PRICE ISN'T THE ONLY THING

Building businesses is an arduous process, while ruining them is child's play. Ultimately, you want the buyer to be happy with the business they've bought and for the profits to remain stable or grow. You want the workforce to continue to be happy coming to work. Part of any deal might require a smooth handover and part of the negotiation will relate to who stays on and for how long. Do they need you for a few months, a year or two, or not at all? If profits collapse, even if it's through no fault of your own, unscrupulous lawyers will be more tempted to scour the sale and purchase agreement to see if there's any money they can recover from shareholders because of a breach of warranty.

EARN-OUT OR NOT?

Earn-outs are a type of deal where you get some money on completion and a further dollop down the line dependent on future profits. They're a good idea in principle, but the majority of earn-outs don't fulfil the expectations of either the acquirer or the seller. If you're selling a growing business and are able to take advantage and get paid now for subsequent years' growth, then an earn-out could work wonders for you, but if your involvement has ended and the price is contingent on profits or costs that you can no longer control, then that's an entirely different story. If you do enter into one of these deals, it's advisable to try and ring-fence your ability to run the business for the period of any earn-out with agreed budgets and minimal interference.

PLAN YOUR COMMUNICATION

Whether you're buying or selling, well planned, clear communication that explains the business rationale, anticipates questions and emphasises the benefits of the transaction can be the difference between a slick sale and an awkward one.

This communication should be planned and rehearsed with military precision, not run like a school play. Both parties only have one chance to make a first impression. Think about the logistics of the communication: whether you'll tell everybody at the same time, how you'll let your customers know.

Proper communication may even have an impact on profits.

When people have pride in the brand they work for, a change of owners can be an emotional event and can create fear, uncertainty and doubt. It's an unsettling time for everybody, and people will need more reassurance than you realise (unless you're an ogre and they can't wait to see the back of you). Repetition of the key messages helps. Tell them four times in four different ways and they might remember half of what you've said.

Here's the psychology behind it. People go through four phases when they hear of a sale – in a way, it's quite similar to mourning:

- Denial: 'How could you do such a thing and why didn't you tell me?'

- Resistance: 'I'm not going to work for these clowns.'

- Exploration: 'Hmmm, maybe there's something in it for me.'

- Commitment: 'Sounds great. Where are we headed next?'

Most staff are unable to skip any of these phases and need to process each part of the cycle, at their own pace, before they can move onto the next phase.

Once this process has been completed, you must be prepared to answer any and all of the questions they ask, both publicly and privately, anticipating as many of them as you can think of in advance. You should also prepare yourself for the reality that assumptions made by employees will initially be negative. Initial questions are likely to be born out of worry. Are there going to be redundancies? What are the culture changes? What will happen to my career development? Will my employment terms change?

It's only when these fears are allayed that staff can consider the benefits the deal might bring.

Your allies in this process can be the middle managers in the company, since they tend to be the real influencers of your business. Prepare to explain things to them at first, get them on side with the whole process, and they can do some of the heavy lifting for you.

AND FINALLY

Remember that if you stay on for any period of time, your relationship with your staff will change. Some of them may be happy for you, but others will begrudge your success. Regardless of this, be proud of your achievement. Take the champagne out of the fridge and share it. People like to be part of a success story.

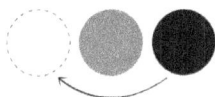

BUYING
A BUSINESS

"IT'S ABOUT TIME WE STOPPED BUYING
THINGS WE DON'T NEED WITH MONEY
WE DON'T HAVE TO IMPRESS PEOPLE WE
DON'T LIKE."

Adrian Rogers

Building a business can be a rewarding way to make money, although going through the process from scratch always costs more than you initially think, and it usually takes longer than you imagine. I always use the rule of two and three: if your venture costs twice as much to break even as you initially think and takes three times as long, will it still be worthwhile?

If the answer is yes, give it the green light. Building business is often like building an extension on your house: very worthwhile in the long term, but it always costs more at the start, and sometimes it's easier to buy an existing business and improve it instead.

Buying a business may initially seem more expensive than building one, but it does give a higher chance of success, since someone else has already proved that the business model works.

UNCERTAINTY AND TARGETING

There are risks and an amount of uncertainty associated with purchasing any business, but so long as you've done enough due diligence, you should know on day one how much you're paying and how much profit it's making. Sometimes you can borrow some of the money and, occasionally, the vendor might let you pay over a period of time. Leveraged finance is the eighth wonder of the world. If you're clever, you can pay for the entire purchase price over time, out of the money you've borrowed and profits the business makes.

What's not to like? It appears to be a licence to print money and sometimes it is – unless you screw it up. That is why you need all the help contained in the Scale section to give yourself the best chance of success.

It's at this time that you will need the help of financing specialists who are experts in their field to hold your hand. Financing can be straightforward, or it can be complex. At the difficult end, you may need to walk through a minefield of understanding such concepts as senior debt, junior debt, mezzanine financing, invoice discounting, warrants, bonds, convertible loans, coupons and more. This is when the experience of one of the NEDs we discussed earlier can help you.

It's sensible to target a business that is already profitable, or at least one that is fully operational. Often a fresh pair of eyes can give a tired business a new lease of life and you can take advantage of the potential. The purchase price may seem high initially; it's usually based on a multiple of the annual earnings before interest and tax (EBIT), less any debt the company has; or alternatively the value of the balance sheet (the amount you'd realise if the business closed down and all the assets were sold off). However, multiples can vary enormously: from double or triple the profits at the lower end for a small business where the perception is that growth is difficult and earnings may not be supported by repeat business, to 10–12 times annual profits for more reliable, fast-growing businesses with experienced management teams and repeatable earnings. Some dotcom businesses aren't profitable and are valued at a multiple of their revenue. A company is ultimately only worth what someone else is prepared to buy it for, so work out what you can afford and stick to it. Be pragmatic. Don't get carried away, as many people do in bidding situations. It's not eBay. Keep your emotion out of it and stick to the plan.

A word of warning: don't give any personal guarantees to the bank, if you can help it, when you're borrowing money from them. They will often ask, but please try to resist the tempta-

"

KEEP YOUR EMOTION OUT

OF IT AND STICK TO THE PLAN.

"

tion. In the unlikely event that things do go wrong, losing the element of money you've put in will be painful enough, without you having to sell personal assets as well (including, in extreme cases, your house). Since my 21st birthday, I've made it a rule never to give a personal guarantee, even if it means losing a deal or moving to a different lender.

SO FAR SO GOOD, BUT NOW IT'S TIME TO BURST YOUR BUBBLE

You have probably heard the expression *caveat emptor*. It's a Latin phrase which means 'Let the buyer beware'.

What you buy usually isn't as good as you'd hoped, even if you've done your diligence thoroughly. Usually, the bigger the business, the more complex it is and the more it costs. Like a fancy wristwatch, there are more things that can go wrong. That's why sometimes it pays to use an outside firm to conduct due diligence on your behalf. Although it'll be expensive, they'll have more experience than you do, and you can usually sue them if they get it wrong and miss something that you had relied on to calculate the value of the business.

Globally, companies spend in excess of $2tn[5] on acquisitions every year. Yet there are countless studies telling us that most people are disappointed with what they buy. The consensus is that the failure rate of mergers and acquisitions ranks somewhere between 70 and 90%[6]. This is clearly a worrying figure and there are many reasons for it. These include poor buying decisions and unprepared managers who aren't able to digest what they have bought.

It's important to emphasise that these are statistics for big companies; while you might expect big companies to make sound decisions, they often drop clangers and get things wrong. It's quite usual for large corporations to make acquisitions for completely the wrong reasons. They may be under pressure from third parties to spend cash. Often, they are egged on by greedy shareholders, who later regret their avarice. Large companies have egos of their own and it's easy to be bold when you're spending other people's money.

In some cases, they may buy competitors and close them down. In other cases, the cultures of both sides are so different and embedded that it's impossible to combine them. I once attended a completion party where two very big businesses came together. I noticed that most of the staff from one side arrived by taxi, while the majority from the other side came by public transport. You didn't need a crystal ball to predict that the merger would be a disaster – and it was. The deal should never have been done.

BUSINESS BROKERS

Well-paid brokers, bankers and corporate finance houses tempt us with aggressive financial projections which are often unrealistic and factor in cost savings that never materialise. Their fees are usually paid by the seller, so they've had time to groom the company and adjust the numbers. They write a marketing document called a sales memorandum which puts the best spin on everything. It's a document you should be suspicious of. There's an expression I've heard for dressing up a company for sale: 'putting lipstick on the pig'. Advisors only get paid if a deal is done, so they don't particularly care whether or not it's a success. It's much easier to keep your feet on the ground if you're writing the cheque yourself.

NOT AN IDEAL OUTCOME

Nonetheless, I'm the first to admit that I've been caught out myself on more than one occasion. It's quite easy to be seduced by a glittering proposition from the outside, when a more pragmatic view would have revealed the truth.

One occasion where I screwed up a business purchase particularly stands out. I was buying a business in the healthcare sector, which looked to be an ideal acquisition at first glance. The business was established and profitable, and it seemed there would be some cost savings, because I already owned a similar business; areas like the compliance team and the accounts department could be combined.

We entered into due diligence to investigate the company before purchasing it, and because I already knew how the business worked, I resisted using outside accountants to help, thinking I could save money by doing it myself. I discovered that the company's earnings were extremely consistent due to its ongoing contracts for supplying doctors and nurses to a variety of NHS hospitals and the private sector.

Everything appeared above board and rosy, and we were looking forward to sprinkling our pixie dust on the business and growing it quickly. We couldn't wait to invest in new systems and had begun to hire new staff in order to bolster the teams at the business. We paid the broker in full.

Things went wrong quite quickly. It became apparent when we started working with them that some of the locum staff had false names and that their identities were misleading. We immediately conducted an extensive audit of the entire business, beginning right from the very bottom. As part of this process, we asked all staff to confirm their identities and prove their qualifications. We hit a brick wall.

We found that 82% of the staff were either non-compliant or had forged documentation. Many were nurses working at hospitals without any legal right to do so. The former owners had believed they were merely bending the rules, when in reality they were committing a major fraud.

All staff had to be revalidated or withdrawn. And we weren't talking here about a personal assistant or two who had exaggerated their keyboard speed – these were healthcare professionals dealing with people's lives. There wasn't a moment to lose; clients needed to be informed. Profits collapsed. Legal proceedings for a warranty claim were commenced against the vendors, but shortly afterwards the company was closed. The brand was tainted. We managed to switch some of the business to our existing brand, but in reality the entire acquisition had been a disaster, and we lost our money.

Looking back at the process, there is a lot that I could have done differently, but ultimately it is impossible to predict every conceivable issue. There are too many rocks to peer under. Fraudsters are clever people and are experts at hiding things and forging documents. If you do enough acquisitions, the chances are that you will get one wrong every now and again. Let the buyer beware.

When it works, though, it's great – and, as with most things, thorough planning can tilt the odds of success. What follows isn't meant to be an exhaustive checklist of things to look out for when buying a business, but it's a good start. Naturally, you'll need to tailor the list to your own particular set of circumstances.

INFORMATION, REFERENCES AND CUSTOMER CONCENTRATION

You can never acquire too much information about your target. Some of it is readily available and some can be found by stealth.

One of the best ways to gather information is to engage in your own silent shopping. Become a customer. Purchase products or services from the company you hope to buy. Experience the customer journey that other consumers will go through, and familiarise yourself with the business as a whole. There is no better way to feel the potential, or lack thereof, of a particular business than buying from it.

Ask the seller for references and pay attention to the ones they give you. If they're not current or from regular, sizeable customers, be suspicious. The seller may just have lined up mates to help them along their sale journey.

Look at customer concentration. If a single customer accounts for over 10% of revenue, it's a problem – and if there's 20% of the business with one customer, it's a big problem. With the way business metrics work, sometimes, if you lose 20% of your sale, it could reduce almost all of your profit.

Trawl websites like Glassdoor to see how happy the business's employees are, and analyse sites like Trustpilot, Trip Advisor or any other review sites you can find to see how happy the customers are. Talk to their competitors, interview their staff, see if there's any market intel about their sector. Look for their track record in legal disputes and see if they are to blame.

We talked in the last chapter about the merits and pitfalls of earn-outs when selling a business. The same applies when buying one. Decide if you want the management team to stay on for a handover period or if you want to link any payments to the business's future profitability.

Staffing will also have a massive impact on the potential success of the business. You should make every effort to ascertain whether there are any union problems at the company, or if there are difficulties with staff generally. Is the culture one you can embrace? Is there a can-do attitude among the workforce?

Hidden factors

Taxes and accounts can also be a major issue. Ensure that these are up to date, and get warranties if claims are made. Tax authorities can go back twenty years and make a claim for unpaid taxes, so you should insist that those warranties should last for the same time period.

Diligence and compliance

There's been an avalanche of compliance and regulation since I started my first business in the wild west. Make sure the business you are buying is thoroughly compliant, with all laws and regulations followed – from safe working conditions to employment contracts and pensions. We can go on and on. Regulation of data, up-to-date filing of accounts, diversity programmes, equal pay and so on. Make sure that your directors' and officers' insurance is adequate and in place. There are skeletons in every cupboard, and your job is to find them.

It normally takes two audit cycles to flush everything out.

MANAGING YOUR BUSINESS

Once you've bought it, with any luck you'll file all the purchase documents in the bottom of a filing cabinet, kiss goodbye to the seller and never look at them again.

It's now time to run the business. It's just like buying a new car; it'll take time to learn how everything works, where things are and what they do. Before long, you'll be well aware of its power, its limitations, how quickly it can change direction, how to handle it and where the brakes are.

The communication around the announcement, internally and externally, that we discussed in the last chapter is even more important when you're the buyer, since you have to pick up the pieces and convince the workforce and your customers that they want to work with you.

THE FIRST 100 DAYS

Before you complete the purchase, have a plan for the first 100 days. Consider your own skills and those of the team you've bought. Make sure you think through all eventualities. Look for quick wins, things to celebrate, reminders to staff and customers that things are going well. Make sure that they do go well. Just like when you're starting a business, if you're doing it properly, there's no work–life balance at the beginning. Listen for the weak signals and fix things quickly; don't let small issues fester.

When it does go well, it's a beautiful thing. You've paid off the purchase price using the company's profits and you still own it. The enormous amount of effort and energy you've put in is absolutely worthwhile. The rewards can be extraordinary; the goal of achieving financial security for life is wonderful and the stress involved can eventually be replaced with true happiness and fulfilment. The very best of luck to you.

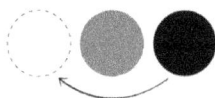

DON'T LET YOUR FLOAT SINK

"IT TAKES JUST ONE WAVE TO CAPSIZE A BOAT, AND ONE MORE TO TAKE IT DOWN."

Federico Chini

F loating your business on the stock exchange isn't for everyone. The costs involved are enormous, the compliance is debilitating and, unless your business is making at least £20m a year and growing, I wouldn't recommend it.

There are great rewards available, though. I've floated two companies on different stock exchanges. I sold one of them for 10 times the float price after just a few short years and delisted the other one. I've been involved in two others that were already listed. I've also floated an interest-bearing bond on another UK exchange. Floating can be a way to de-risk, but you shouldn't see it as a sale, even though you might be able to take some money out at the time of the public offering. It's a way to raise funds to grow and fund acquisitions. It's also the biggest fee frenzy you're ever likely to see in your lifetime. The fees could be as much as 10% of the money you raise – and don't forget, you're paying all of them. Fix or cap fees whenever you can, or costs can spiral out of control. When you add up the hourly rates of all the people attending some of the big round-table meetings you have, it's not unusual for the combined rate to be more than £10k for a couple of hours' discussion.

This chapter represents a 12-point guide to some of the most important issues I've encountered when engaging in flotation. I sincerely hope it will expose what happens under the kimono.

WHY FLOAT?

The first thing to address is your motivation for floating a company in the first place. What are your reasons for doing so? Do you know what you're letting yourself in for? Do you have an idea about the level of money you'll raise and the value attributed to you at the time you float? That will tell you the dilution you will take to your shareholding. Do you know what the expectations of new investors might be? Do they want you to pay a dividend, or will they just expect higher capital growth? Will being a public company stifle your entrepreneurial personality? When you're on this treadmill, predicted profit forecasts must be hit and investors will expect routine progress, not fits and starts. You will be reporting your numbers every six months, or quarterly in some cases. Will that suit your business or your management style?

If you thought you were burdened with paperwork and compliance before your float, think again. Running a public company is another level of administration altogether and, should anything go wrong, you really will be washing your dirty linen in public. There will be a committee to set your salary, another committee to manage the audit and a third one to look after the nomination of new board members.

Have I put you off yet?

As well as the stratospheric costs at the beginning, there are ongoing costs. Auditors and lawyers will charge more because your risk profile is higher. The cost of preparing accounts will be higher, and then there's the annual report to design, print and distribute. A PR company will need to be retained to communicate with investors; your marketing team will need to up their game to reflect your status, too. There's the cost of extra NEDs. Announcements will need to be written, checked by lawyers, published and distributed. I could go on…

The extra ongoing annual costs of running a small public company can easily be £500k or more, without even blinking.

Perhaps more important than the annual costs is the value of your time that will get snaffled with investors, road shows, phone calls from brokers, the regulator, shareholders and journalists. You will get invited to awaydays, awards dinners and golf days. I've never been a fan of golf. I can't see the point, especially given the weather in this country; it's like dogging but without the sex or the car.

Surely I've put you off by now?

There are plenty of alternatives to flotation. Consider taking on senior bank debt, mezzanine finance, accounts receivable finance, or even a private equity partner. This latter arrangement will see the partner buy part of your business and provide finance to fund growth plans. Although there's likely to be more accountability to your partner, you'll still be able to run the business in the way you agree to run it.

Flotations can be highly attractive, but the right conditions need to exist in order for them to be worthwhile and right for your business.

DISTRACTION LIMITATION

Even the simplest flotation of the smallest company will suck up an enormous amount of a senior manager's time. It wouldn't take much for them to take their eye off their main job, which is to run the business on a day-to-day basis and look after its profits.

There's nothing worse than disappointing the market. If your business has lost focus on its main aim – profit – then the first time you ever report your accounts after your initial public offering (IPO), you'll look like an amateur and shareholders won't trust you for a long time until you redeem yourself.

With this in mind, it is imperative to have one point of contact who is responsible for the float. If necessary, hire in the experience of a non-executive or some kind of interim help. You will need assistance when undertaking this process.

THE BARBER SYNDROME

During the process, it can be very difficult to acquire good-quality independent advice. The issue here is that most of the people who understand the market are the very people who will gain financially from the process, so they're not independent. It's a bit like asking a barber whether you need a haircut. The answer will usually be, yes sir, of course you do.

So where do you go for independent counsel on this issue?

Speak to people who have done it before. Hopefully one of your NEDs can advise you. Use your network. Be prepared to contact the chief executive of a recently floated company. I have always found them to be very receptive and they can provide a valuable insight into the whole process. It's illuminating to speak to someone who has experienced in the recent past the very thing that you're considering.

CHOOSE THE RIGHT MARKET

When you're floating a company, it is essential to aim for the most appropriate market. There are options. Should you be heading for AIM, which is a junior market for smaller companies where the reporting requirements are less? Or maybe the London Stock Exchange, or one of the overseas bourses from America or Hong Kong? It depends on your size, type of business, where your customers are, and which market understands you best.

CHOOSE THE RIGHT HELP

You'll be working with a raft of advisors, so pick people you can obtain references for or who have been recommended (not by other advisors; they all play the back-scratching game). Meet the partners, choose people you like and get along with. You will be spending a lot of time with them, so don't pick people who irritate you. There are lots of them about, especially in the City.

Brokers also need to provide quality research in your sector; they really need to know their stuff. You should seek out advisors who have strong competencies in the areas you particularly require, rather than people who might be high profile, well known or deemed particularly successful. This may sometimes require you to step on some toes; your friendly auditor may have to go, as a trade-off of cost versus credibility.

GET LIQUID

If you're a small company with a market capitalisation of less than £250m and little prior market experience, you can be certain that there will be virtually no liquidity in your stock. This will make it extremely difficult for any members of staff or directors to buy or sell chunks of stock without affecting the share price, which is not a desirable outcome.

The only solution to this problem is to get bigger, which will lead to more trades and a tighter spread (the difference between the buy and sell prices). Market-makers move the price up or down to hustle trade, not to suit you, or even to reflect reality. The market has never been a rational reflection of reality; it always reflects investment activity.

CORPORATE GOVERNANCE

I can't over-emphasise the issue of corporate governance and how expensive and time consuming it is. While I do believe that it's absolutely essential to protect the rights and interests of share-holders, I also believe the pendulum has swung too far towards mollycoddling investors who know the risks, and discourages the informed risk-taking that shareholders expect.

ESTIMATES AND FORECASTS

When it comes to estimating and forecasting, there is an extremely simple rule of thumb: always under-promise and over-deliver. For the first three reporting periods after a flota-tion, you will find yourself in 'show me' mode. It is up to you to demonstrate to the wider investment community that your com-pany always delivers the results you promise. You'll be rewarded with a higher valuation and, if you need to raise more money, people who trust you will often back you.

NON-EXECUTIVE DIRECTORS

Non-executive directors can be extremely valuable for any company, as I discussed extensively in the chapter on NEDs, and they can assist with a flotation and beyond. Select the right people for the right job, though, and target the best talent. Reference them in the same way you would any other key member of staff. Don't keep them for long enough that they can go stale. If you search hard enough, you may find one who can use their contacts to bring business into your company.

INSIDER DEALING

Limit staff access to information that is market sensitive. Be obsessive about confidentiality, making sure emails and accounts files are secure and password protected. Rumours spread quickly, and some unscrupulous staff might be tempted to use information they've stumbled across to buy shares directly, or through contacts they know.

That is insider dealing, and it can result in big fines or jail time. Many entrepreneurs love bragging about their successes and will talk endlessly about customers they have won and profits they are making. You can't even hint about this in the public arena, or you could go directly to Jail, without passing Go or collecting £200. Put a sock in it.

FORGET LOYALTY

There isn't much loyalty among shareholders. Despite their encouraging praise at investor meetings, some of them will buy, sell or trade your shares if they can make a profit from doing so.

Hedge funds are well known for this. Don't get upset; that's just the way it is.

Institutional investors are different. They will often take bigger stakes if they believe in your long-term plan, and support you through your journey. Cultivate these relationships well. Even in the racy world of high finance, people still buy from people they like and trust.

DIVIDEND POLICY

If you're engaging in a flotation, you will inevitably be asked about your dividend policy. Talk to your advisors and devise a policy that you can sensibly articulate, even if that policy is not to pay a dividend for a number of years. What you decide will depend on how much money the business is throwing off and what you plan to do with it. Some investment funds rely on it, while others don't care. Your policy will define the sort of investor who gets involved, though.

One final thought on the subject of shares is that it is extremely unwise to borrow against your own personal shares. It can be a very tempting proposition and there are banks who will lend against that security, but something unexpected can happen and the share price can collapse. Not only will you have lost any value in the shares then, but you may not be able to pay back the bank for money you've already spent. That holiday home in Barbados will then have to wait.

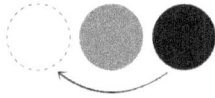

PHILANTHROPY - THE PARADOX OF GENEROSITY

**"WE MAKE A LIVING BY WHAT WE GET;
WE MAKE A LIFE BY WHAT WE GIVE."**

P hilanthropy and big business go hand in hand in modern society. Those who pay attention to the media will see regular examples of this. However, there is a lot going on beneath the surface that might not immediately be apparent.

Helping your community and giving back to society isn't just a kind act; it actually benefits your business as well. Staff nowadays, and investors too, want to know what your corporate responsibility plan is and whether they can identify with it. With this in mind, whether you're an individual or acting on behalf of a corporate body, it's sensible to involve your staff and let them have some input into who you are giving your money and time to, and what you are giving. It's another strand of the company's cultural DNA. It's sensible to build this ethic and the practice of philanthropy into your business culture right from the very start.

GIVING AND RECEIVING

Do you remember when you were growing up that there came a time where you got more pleasure out of giving presents than receiving them?

With corporate giving, there are plenty of reasons why your company can benefit even more than the cause you are supporting. That sounds like a win-win situation in anyone's language.

There are not many of us who haven't benefited from the help of others at some point in our lives; being able to assist those less fortunate than ourselves is not just a worthwhile cause in its own right, but one that benefits the image and reputation of your company, too. If that doesn't convince you, let your accountant know that you generally receive tax relief on the amount of the gift!

Being committed to corporate giving can assist your business in a number of ways:

- It can build trust in your brand.

- The charitable initiatives on your website can become an integral part of your culture and give third-party affirmation that you are reliable and ethical.

- It can boost employee morale.

- It can define your culture.

- It can increase your reach to a wider audience.

- It can help you to have an active influence in your own community.

PILLAR OF THE COMMUNITY

Companies tend to be set up to make a profit, which is of course perfectly natural. However, it is also important to remember that our businesses do not function in isolation from the communities that surround them.

This means that it doesn't necessarily take a huge effort to rally the whole neighbourhood behind you in a way that advertising could never achieve. Both you and your staff could be working shoulder to shoulder with a wider audience, fighting a worthy cause and also elevating the image of your business in the collective mind of the local community.

Those involved in philanthropy projects often talk about a 'helper's high' or a 'giver's glow'. There's a warm feeling associated with assisting others – and in terms of business, this is very much a reciprocal relationship. People usually choose to work with people and brands that they admire and trust. There is no better way to build this admiration than by showing that you care about life beyond simply turning a profit.

DIFFERENT MOTIVATIONS

People feel the need to give their money and time for a variety of very personal reasons; if you're fundraising from your staff to augment your company's contribution, you might be interested to see what those reasons are. I've cribbed this list from a professional fundraiser I know:

- Giving back is their religious leader's will.

- Some people selfishly work out that they will get more back than they give.

- Others feel the need to repay an institution or hospital after a life-changing event.

- For some, it's a family tradition going back for generations.

- Others enjoy the fun and social element.

- Some people are naturally altruistic and it just feels right.

- A small number crave recognition and want to see their name in lights.

Regardless of the reasons, the outcome of helping others is compelling and can benefit your business significantly. There is a genuine convergence of interests at the heart of the process.

OILING THE WHEELS

Engaging in philanthropy oils the wheels of commerce. Thankfully, many (but not enough) communities have examples of those who have benefited as a consequence of corporate giving – from local taxi firms to retailers, from sole traders to international brands.

At one end of the spectrum, I met the owner of a café in the East End of London who had learned sign language to better communicate with a profoundly deaf couple who were among his customers. He was rewarded with an unintended consequence: more than a hundred pupils of the school where they taught began eating in his establishment on a regular basis.

At the other end of the spectrum, the Bill and Melinda Gates Foundation has brought enormous benefits to mankind and saved millions of lives, having donated over $45bn to their chosen causes over the last 20 years. It has been argued that this apparently altruistic act has also had the sinister consequence of buying them power and influence. That viewpoint is difficult to dispute; money and power buy influence, even in philanthropic settings.

Despite the seedier side of giving, it's encouraging to observe the trend of the super-rich pledging large chunks of their wealth to charitable causes while they are still alive. The Giving Pledge, which is a campaign to encourage extremely wealthy people to contribute a majority of their wealth to philanthropic causes, has attracted pledges of an estimated $600bn from over 200 of the world's richest people.

MEASURING THE BENEFIT

There are many ways of measuring the hard and soft benefits of working with people who need our help. Staff retention, for example, can be measured. Staff morale can be evaluated. Social media posts and likes can be seen by everyone.

'Non-sales opportunities' can be measured, as well; for example, being asked to feature in video interviews, invitations to speak on conference panels, or opportunities to become involved in the running of not-for-profit businesses – essentially, anything that makes you and your business more visible. Finally, regular staff surveys can measure the overall contentment of the workforce, so you can get tangible feedback on how they view the company and the impact that your philanthropic efforts are having on morale. Not everything in life is measured by profit – sometimes it just feels good to do the right thing.

We all will have our own treasured causes, and one of the great benefits of owning your own business is that you can use your corporate might to help the people you feel most passionate about or the areas where you can make the most difference.

In my own case, I've tried to use the skills I've developed to help people working in the arts. For me, that's involved mentoring, coaching and supporting individuals who have benefited from the addition of structure, some financial support, and an unerring belief linked to a well-thought-out plan. Failure is so much more of a sensitive issue for artists, since any rejection is felt personally, as opposed to any thicker-skinned corporate failure. Artists can be delicate souls and their confidence more fragile. Perhaps I recognise a reflection of my own insecurity, especially from the early part of my career. Many business owners I have met aren't the tough nuts they are made out to be. They have a similar combination of a fear of failure and an iron will to succeed.

If someone is too tired to give you a smile, leave one of your own; no one needs a smile as much as those who have none to give.

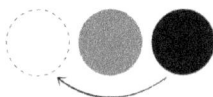

ENJOY THE PRIZE

"ONCE YOU'VE ACHIEVED ALL OF YOUR GOALS, WHAT WILL YOU WISH FOR?"

Gary Ashworth

If you knew that all of your goals were achievable, what would you wish for?

Imagine it's the day after you've sold your business. An enormous sum of money is sitting in your bank account, and you have achieved financial security for the rest of your life, for both you and your family. That would be a pretty blissful experience. You can't stop grinning from ear to ear. You never have to work again unless you choose to do so. You can spend the rest of your life doing what you want to do, not what you have to do.

LIFE CHOICES

Many of the things you dreamed about as you beavered away along the journey are now within your sight. You've arrived. This is the place you have been craving for all these years.

Once you sell a business for a material amount of money, it gives you choices. I know this feeling; I've done it myself several times. What will you do next? How will you reinvest yourself?

Do you want to pay off your mortgage or buy a bigger house? Perhaps you could buy a boat, a ski chalet, or even a private jet. You could go travelling anywhere and everywhere, staying in the best hotels or exclusive homes, experiencing all of the world's greatest luxuries. You could spend more time at home with your family and friends.

Or you could become a philanthropist and start a foundation. You could apply the skills you've learned to something else. You could become a coach, mentor or consultant, assisting others with the challenging process of becoming successful. You have the choice to make a massive difference or do nothing at all.

My first big sale was Abacus Recruitment PLC, the accountancy and IT staffing business. I had started the company when I was 21, and I floated it on the stock market to great success, as mentioned previously. Once this process was completed, I felt punch drunk, but I knew deep down that as long as I didn't do anything stupid with the money, I had achieved financial security for life for both myself and my children.

EMOTIONAL DRAIN

When you first sell a business, particularly if you have been involved with it for several years, there will inevitably be a period of adjustment. It may surprise you, but you may feel awkward for a little while, because for so long you have been defined by the business you have run and suddenly it's not there any more. Handing your baby over to someone else can be an exhausting wrench. It can be difficult to let go. There's a feeling of loss.

You may encounter seller's remorse. It can be a grieving process for families. Many of your former employees have become friends, and your relationship with them will change now you're no longer their boss. This loss of your identity can even lead to depression, but it's difficult to talk to anyone because, from an outsider's point of view, you have everything in the world that you could possibly wish for. You've won the lottery and shouldn't have anything to worry about.

Equally, there can be concerns that other people will just see the money in the bank and feel jealous of your success. Some of your new-found friends may not be as genuine as you hope!

Talk to other business owners who have sold their companies. They will no doubt reassure you that – although there may be a period of adjustment – once you've decided what the next part of your life journey will be, you regain a sense of purpose, and the excitement builds again.

NOT AGAIN!

More people than you might realise have bought their businesses back after the people they sold them to screwed them up. Michael Birch, the tech entrepreneur, sold Bebo.com to AOL for $595m in 2008. This was later considered to be one of the worst deals in the dotcom bubble. AOL didn't understand the market or the nature of the business they had purchased (Bebo was a precursor to Facebook and could have been great); consequently, they ruined the business completely. Birch eventually bought it back for $1m.

Anyway, enjoy the prize – you've earned it. I hope some of the things you've read in this book will encourage you and inspire you. Starting, scaling and selling a business can be great fun and very rewarding. If you've not started yet and are teetering on the edge, wondering whether you should start or buy a business, I hope my words might just push you over the edge and encourage you to go for it.

Carpe diem – seize the day.

CONCLUSION

This is the end product of all of your hard work. This is the point where you have a clear vision of whether you want to keep your business, sell it, or hand it over to somebody else. You'll have a clear strategy of how to groom the business for sale and an understanding of what the process is likely to be like. You might be thinking of what you'll do next, what difference the cash will make to you, or what difference you will make to other people's lives as a consequence of your achievement.

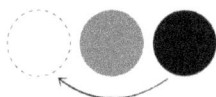

GOOD LUCK!

Right. That's it. I've done my part. Now it's over to you.

I've told you all I know – which isn't everything, but it's enough of a recipe for you to follow and be successful. Thousands of businesses have been started, scaled and sold in this manner, and there's no reason why you can't own the next successful one.

Let me know how you get on; I'm interested to hear your journey. Indeed, if you're happy for me to do so, I'll share your story on my website where we can form a community to help each other.

There is a lot to consider and the best way to figure out specifically what needs to be done in your business is with outside help. Someone with an external perspective whose only focus is to get you closer to your end goal. Someone that doesn't come with the emotion or baggage of growing up with your company. Someone who has seen and done it all before and can help you do the same.

This is exactly what I do with my clients.

If you would like to explore how I can work with you to achieve the same level of success in your business get in touch at:
www.garyashworth.com/eatthepuddingfirst

Let's eat the pudding together!

ACKNOWLEDGEMENTS

Thank you to all the people who have helped and influenced me so far on my journey. If I've plagiarised any of your sayings or techniques, then I apologise; it wasn't intentional. I've been in business for enough time now not to remember where I learned everything from.

The following people deserve a mention. There's a tiny part of all of them in me.

Luke, Chris and Ben, James, Phil and Suzie, Dave Ed, Lottie, Geoff, Paul Williams, Russ, David Higgins, Nick Dog, Dodo, Slick, Sir George, Karl, Lottie, Elias, Harry Sandercock, Boothby, Ledders, Jonathan Buckle, Moz, Mark Farlow, Chris Morris, Bonzo, Jan and Balls, Plops, Becca, Alan and Michael, Java, Romney, Keith and Jean, John and Alex. Diane and Jeanette, Margo, John the Greek (the man, not the horse), Tony and Pam, Mellon Man, Nick Wells, Alan Perriam, Robert Dilts, David Johnson and John MacKay, Mrs Back, Hoola, Leila and Ali, Davina for inspiring me to pick up the project again, and Olivia for giving me the courage to keep going. The lyrics on the *Born to Run* album and the bar of the Groucho Club.

The writing of these people also helped me more than I care to admit: Stephen Covey, Jim Collins, Tom Peters, Neil Rackham, Daniel Burrus, William Bridges, Bob Thomas at Ashridge, Peter Senge, Gregory Bateson, Malcolm Gladwell, Burt Bacharach, Robert Kiyosaki, Meredith Belbin, Peter Druker, Daniel Goleman, Charles Handy.

ENDNOTES

1 https://www.lsbf.org.uk/press-and-media/news-about-lsbf/2015/september-2015/lsbf-careers-report-finds-that-47-of-uk-workforce-want-a-career-change

2 https://hbr.org/2015/03/technology-can-save-onboarding-from-itself

3 https://globalstudies.unc.edu/wp-content/uploads/sites/224/2013/11/Wilen-Cora-The-95.pdf

4 https://www.todaysdietitian.com/newarchives/111114p36.shtml

5 https://www.reuters.com/article/us-markets-m-a-idUSKCN1IN2C0

6 https://hbr.org/2016/06/ma-the-one-thing-you-need-to-get-right